WITHDRAW

WORN, SOILED, OBSOLETE

D0523428

GAMES AND ACTIVITIES FOR ATTACHING WITH YOUR CHILD

by the same author

Attaching Through Love, Hugs and Play
Simple Strategies to Help Build Connections with Your Child
Deborah D. Gray
ISBN 978 1 84905 939 8
eISBN 978 0 85700 753 7

Attaching in Adoption
Practical Tools for Today's Parents
Deborah D. Gray
ISBN 978 1 84905 890 2
eISBN 978 0 85700 606 6

Nurturing Adoptions
Creating Resilience after Neglect and Trauma
Deborah D. Gray
ISBN 978 1 84905 891 9
eISBN 978 0 85700 607 3

of related interest

Attachment in Common Sense and Doodles
A Practical Guide
Miriam Silver
ISBN 978 1 84905 314 3
eISBN 978 0 85700 624 0

A Short Introduction to Attachment and Attachment Disorder
Colby Pearce
ISBN 978 1 84310 957 0
eISBN 978 1 84642 949 1
Part of the JKP 'Short Introductions' series

Creating Loving Attachments
Parenting with PACE to Nurture Confidence and Security in the Troubled Child
Kim S. Golding and Daniel A. Hughes
ISBN 978 1 84905 227 6
eISBN 978 0 85700 470 3

Reparenting the Child Who Hurts
A Guide to Healing Developmental Trauma and Attachments
Caroline Archer and Christine Gordon
Foreword by Gregory C. Keck, Ph.D.
ISBN 978 1 84905 263 4
eISBN 978 0 85700 568 7

GAMES AND ACTIVITIES FOR ATTACHING WITH YOUR CHILD

Deborah D. Gray and Megan Clarke

Jessica Kingsley *Publishers*
London and Philadelphia

First published in 2015
by Jessica Kingsley Publishers
73 Collier Street
London N1 9BE, UK
and
400 Market Street, Suite 400
Philadelphia, PA 19106, USA

www.jkp.com

Copyright © Deborah D. Gray and Megan Clarke 2015
Front cover and book photographs copyright © Doug Manelski 2015

All rights reserved. No part of this publication may be reproduced in any material
form (including photocopying or storing it in any medium by electronic means and
whether or not transiently or incidentally to some other use of this publication)
without the written permission of the copyright owner except in accordance with the
provisions of the Copyright, Designs and Patents Act 1988 or under the terms of a
licence issued by the Copyright Licensing Agency Ltd, Saffron House, 6–10 Kirby
Street, London EC1N 8TS. Applications for the copyright owner's written permission
to reproduce any part of this publication should be addressed to the publisher.

Warning: The doing of an unauthorized act in relation to a copyright work
may result in both a civil claim for damages and criminal prosecution.

Library of Congress Cataloging in Publication Data
Gray, Deborah D., 1951-
   Games and activities for attaching with your child / Deborah D. Gray and Megan Clarke.
      pages cm
   Includes bibliographical references.
   ISBN 978-1-84905-795-0 (alk. paper)
   1. Attachment behavior in children. 2. Parent and child.
3. Educational games. I. Clarke, Megan. II.
Title.
   BF723.A75G734 2015
   649'.5--dc23
                                   2015005270

British Library Cataloguing in Publication Data
A CIP catalogue record for this book is available from the British Library

ISBN 978 1 84905 795 0
eISBN 978 1 78450 152 5

Printed and bound in the United States

Dedications

To Tim, Conor and Coleman, who inspire
me to stretch and grow every day.
Megan Clarke

To Trish, Elise, Zora, Langston and Isaiah, without
whom this wouldn't have been possible, and to my
parents, who taught me about Attachment.
Jill Dziko

To my mom, Becky Fisher, who taught
me the joy of playing games.
Julie Fisher

To the community of children and families
forming attachments after challenges.
Deborah Gray

To Sebastian, Gus and Amelia.
Laura Stone

Contents

ACKNOWLEDGEMENTS   13

Introduction   15

1. Bonds, Attachments, and Play   17
   DEBORAH GRAY
   - Attachment defined   17
   - Security in attachment   19
   - Pleasure, pressures, play, and attachments   21
   - Secure attachments—strong, kind, playful parents and confident kids   23
   - Creating patterns of security after rocky early years   24
   - Wired through our attachments   25
   - Attachment and understanding how people think (theory of mind)   26
   - Emotional "skills" and attachment   27

2. The Value of Play   29
   MEGAN CLARKE
   - Play defined   30
   - Play and your child's development   30
   - The importance of play for parents   32
   - Let's be playful   33

Connecting Through Games

3. Connecting the Two of You   37
   - *Infants and Toddlers*   *37*
   - *Age 3 and Up*   *55*
   - *Age 5 and Up*   *65*

4. Connecting the Whole Family   75

   Infants and Toddlers   *75*

   Age 3 and Up   *89*

5. Connecting Siblings   107

   Age 3 and up   *107*

6. Activities to Help with Mood and Flexibility   115

   All ages   *115*

7. Building Attachment when Children Have Had Exposure
   to Toxins   121
   JILL DZIKO

   Age 5 and up   *125*

   Infants, toddlers and school age   *135*

   ADDENDUM: NOTES FOR PROFESSIONALS   141
   JILL DZIKO   141
   JULIE FISHER   143
   LAURA STONE   145

   BIOGRAPHIES   149

   RESOURCE LIST   151

List of Games and Activities

CONNECTING THE TWO OF YOU

Activity	Age	Participants	Play Time	Page
Airplane ride	18 months to 5 years	Parent and child	1–5 minutes	39
Reverse swinging	Toddler to 8+ years	Parent and child	1–10 minutes	41
"Row, row, row your boat"	Infants/Toddlers	Parent and child	1–10 minutes	43
Piano	Toddlers/Pre-schoolers	Parent and child	2–10 minutes	46
This little piggy	Infants/Toddlers	Parent and child	1–5 minutes	49
Pony boy/girl	Toddler to around 7 years	Parent and child	1–10 minutes	52
Musical chairs	3–7	Parent and child	3–5 minutes	57
Songs about us	3–5	Parent and child	3–5 minutes	59
Paper people	3–5	Parent and child	20–60 minutes	61
Handprints	3–5	Parent and child	3–5 minutes	63
Nose touches	3–5	Parent and child	3–5 minutes	63
Blow bubbles	3–5	Parent and child	3–5 minutes	63
Homemade playdough	3–5	Parent and child	3–5 minutes	63
Watch bugs	3–5	Parent and child	3–5 minutes	63
Face paint	3–5	Parent and child	3–5 minutes	63
Hairdresser	3–5	Parent and child	3–5 minutes	63
Look at clouds	3–5	Parent and child	3–5 minutes	63
Macaroni necklace	3–5	Parent and child	3–5 minutes	63
Roll a ball	3–5	Parent and child	3–5 minutes	63
Go swimming	3–5	Parent and child	3–5 minutes	64

Activity	Age	Participants	Play Time	Page
Selfies	3–5	Parent and child	3–5 minutes	64
Make a mural	5 and up	Parent and one or more children	20–60 minutes	65
Back drawings	5 and up	Parent and one or more children	5–10 minutes	67
Scribble	5 and up	Parent and child	5–10 minutes	69
Child as parent	5 and up	Parent and child	10–30 minutes	71
Writing back and forth	9 and up (including teens)	Parent and child	30 minutes	73

CONNECTING THE WHOLE FAMILY

Activity	Age	Participants	Play Time	Page
Burrito	All ages	Whole family	5–10 minutes	75
Hot dog hugs	All ages	Whole family	1–5 minutes	78
Ball play	Infant to 5 years	Whole family	1–5 minutes	80
"Ring around the rosy"	Toddler to 8 years	Whole family	1–10 minutes	83
Hide-and-seek	All ages	Whole family	5–30 minutes	85
Who is in this family?	3 and up	Whole family	3–5 minutes	89
Family circle	3 and up	Whole family	5–10 minutes	91
Family photo puzzle	5 and up	Whole family	30 minutes	93
Story rounds	5 and up	Whole family	30 minutes	95
Family cookbook	5 and up	Whole family	Varies	97
Quilt of questions	5 and up	Whole family	1 hour to make; 20–30 minutes to play	99
Family pie	5 and up	Whole family	1 hour +	101
Family shield	All ages	Whole family	1–2 hours	104

CONNECTING SIBLINGS

Activity	Age	Participants	Play Time	Page
Forts	3 and up	Siblings	10 minutes to all day	107
Body tracings	5 and up	Siblings	20 minutes	109
The story of…	5 and up	Siblings	10–60 minutes	111
Quests and adventures	5 and up	Siblings	20 minutes to all day	113

ACTIVITIES TO HELP WITH MOOD AND FLEXIBILITY

Activity	Age	Participants	Play Time	Page
Red light, green light	All ages	Three or more	20 minutes	115
Statues	All ages	Group	10 minutes	117
Dance party	All ages	Group	15 minutes	119

WHEN CHILDREN HAVE HAD EXPOSURE TO TOXINS

Activity	Age	Participants	Play Time	Page
Back drawings: Pacing; body space	5 and up	Parent and child	Varies	125
Family cookbook: Connecting the whole family	5–12	Parent and child	Varies	128
Scribble: Connecting the two of you; learning to read/write	5 and up	Whole family	Varies	130
The color of feelings: Connecting the whole family	5 and up	Whole family/ group	Varies	132
This Little Piggy	Infant–Toddler	Parent and child	Varies	135
Family Photo Puzzle	5 and up	Whole family	30 minutes	137

Acknowledgements

Stephen Jones, Senior Commissioning Editor at Jessica Kingsley Publishers, first noticed the need for a book of attachment games. I am so grateful for his ongoing development of a literature that helps parents to create connections with children. As I began to think of the activities that we use to develop secure attachments, I realized how pleasant this book project would be—especially if it were a shared project.

I asked co-editor, Megan Clarke, to join me in the project. She is smart, knowledgeable, flexible, and balanced. What a combination! We thought immediately about three contributors, all accomplished licensed therapists and social workers, whose attachment work includes a delightful amount of play with purpose. Those three, Jill Dziko, Laura Stone, and Julie Fisher, all have the magic combination of being realistic about difficulties that families face, while enjoying the process of attachment-building between children and their families. It has been a pleasure to see their suggestions shine in this book.

As we worked on the games, it became clear that photos would enhance the book. Doug Manelski, a professional photographer, contributed his talent to capture the essence of play and attachment. Thank you, Doug. My thanks, as well, to the cheerful and photogenic volunteers who posed for the photos.

I continue to be blessed by the many supportive people who are part of our community. While I could not name all of them, particular names come to mind. Thank you, Julian Davies, MD, and Julie Bledsoe, MD, co-directors of the Center for Adoption Medicine at the University of Washington and pediatricians with the FASD clinic. We are better practitioners and parents because of you. Michelle Schneidler and Dan Hamer, with ReFRESH, have worked to provide conferences, information and education, parent-to-parent support, and now summer camps for families. I am amazed at the accomplishments, and know that God is at work in your work.

Brian Andersen, with Cascadia Training, continues to provide top-notch training for professionals—and creates community intentionally. These professional communities provide the ongoing support for professionals, so that they stay fresh and support families.

My thanks to Gerald MacKenzie, who conceptualizes this generation's methods of sharing information. My website launch of Nurturingattachments.com will reflect his communication concepts, which build on my books. As always, my thanks to my family. They have consistently valued my work, incorporating my care for families into our family priorities. I am blessed.

Deborah Gray MSW, MPA
Kirkland, WA, 2015

When my co-editor asked me to embark on this project with her, I was elated. Deborah is an incredibly skilled and knowledgeable clinician, as well as a powerful mentor. I have learned a tremendous amount from her and feel blessed to be able to continue learning from her vast experience. She is not only a wise teacher, but a kind and wonderful person.

My colleagues, Jill Dziko, Jill Fisher, and Laura Stone, have been a tremendous source of support and knowledge throughout this entire process. This is a deeply talented group of professionals with whom I always look forward to working and laughing!

I can't thank my husband, Tim, enough. He is my biggest source of support and inspiration, who knew I would someday write a book long before I did. He is my soulmate, the love of my life and the person with whom I have the most fun. My sons, Conor and Coleman, are an incredible source of joy for me. I feel honored to watch them grow and experience the world. I am incredibly proud of the people they are becoming and appreciate all the times they have cheered me on!

Megan Clarke, MA, LMFT
Bellevue, WA, 2015

Introduction

Play seems like such a simple thing, doesn't it? The joy that comes from playing with our children can be a simple joy. Yet, while we are playing, deep connections can be made, changes in relationships can happen, and skills can be mastered. This book is meant to help parents use play to enhance and improve the closeness, or attachment, in your relationship with your children.

We begin the book by discussing the value of attachments—how they influence your child's relationship with you, their understanding of their feelings and those of others. We discuss attachment's contribution to brain-based executive abilities: self-monitoring, inhibition of impulses, understanding the main point of things rather than just the details, and maintaining attention when it takes an effort. The first chapter describes some ways that play enhances the development of these abilities. This discussion gives an overview of both the value of attachment and the ways in which play contributes to attachment—especially in situations where there are challenges.

We then look at the value of play. We live in a busy, busy world where achievement and success are valued and recreation is deemed a luxury. Science is beginning to encourage us to think differently. We explore what makes an activity inherently playful. We then take a look at what a wonderful role imagination and play take in a child's development, as well as the role it can hold in our adult lives. This book is meant to be encouraging. Parenting is a beautiful, yet challenging, journey. As parents ourselves, we understand the demands placed on parents today and encourage you to use this book in a relaxed, playful way.

This book is filled with fun, creative games, crafts, and activities designed to improve closeness between parents and children, siblings, and families as a whole. Most are simple concepts laid out in a clear, approachable way. A description of each activity details what supplies you might need, as well as directions. As there is no absolute right or wrong way to do the activities, each game has alternate suggestions so you can tailor the activity to your child. We want parents to approach these activities with a relaxed sense of joy. This is play, after all!

The final chapter recognizes that parents with children who have had early exposure to toxins may need to approach the activities in a different way. Filled with detailed information and encouraging words, this chapter tailors some of the previous games so parents can slow the pacing down and children can absorb with joy and closeness without being overwhelmed.

This book is a true collaborative work by a group of colleagues who work with children and families challenged by attachment. Truth be told, we also have a tremendous amount of fun working together. Jill Dziko, Julie Fisher, and Laura Stone are talented clinicians who bring warmth and a sense of fun into the work that they do. Working with them was so much fun. We hope you find this book helpful, and above all, that you and your child experience the joy of play and close connections!

Chapter 1

Bonds, Attachments, and Play

DEBORAH GRAY

Let's have fun together! What an appealing way to develop a relationship! Whether you are two years old or 42, our favorite times in life include the magic combination of fun and emotional connection. This book focuses on fun and play as ways to enrich relationships between parents and children, brothers and sisters, and the whole family. Every parent can use a few ideas to enliven their times with their children. This book provides games, activities, and support for parents so that they can engage their children in play.

Play helps you as parents build close ties, or *bonds*, with your children. Very simply, as we play with our children, we bond with them. Whether you are just now forming a bond with your child, or want to improve one, playful bonding times help to build patterns of positive relationships, or quality *attachments*.

ATTACHMENT DEFINED

Parents new to the topic of "bonding" or "attachment" may wonder exactly what is meant by these terms. And what is the difference between the two?

Simply put, bonds are the connections that we have with significant people in our lives. When we share experiences, or have our needs met and meet needs, we form "bonds." These bonds can be with teammates, classmates, teachers, grandparents, and friends. Some of these bonds will be lifelong, some not. In contrast, our attachments can be thought of as "super bonds." Attachments are exclusive—we share our deepest emotions and most personal interactions with special people in our lives. For example, an attached young child wants hugs and lap time with parents, selecting them above others. That child will go on to spend ample time in their parents' presence. That will allow them the confidence to share vulnerabilities and dreams with parents. Throughout childhood they learn to share deeper conversations and experiences with people who are uniquely trusted and know them well—usually parents or grandparents. When missing their parents, children will not be consoled for long by other people or activities. They want the people to whom they are attached, not just any friendly person.

Attachments are usually with people within our immediate families. People to whom we are attached are not replaceable by someone else who is filling in for an absent attachment figure. For example, a neighbor who is helping out for a few days for a mother who is in hospital will not become the child's attachment figure, replacing her mom. She and the child may form a bond. However, if the neighbor continued as a caregiver for a period of many weeks or months, depending on the child's age, that child could gradually form an attachment to the neighbor.

Attachments are typically lifelong. Losing someone we are attached to causes us intense grief. For children, it can cause both physical and emotional disorientation and even loss of speech and motor accomplishments. Attachment loss is a childhood disaster. Children depend on their parents to provide for their emotional equilibrium. Many parents reading this book may have children whose birthparents were unable to care for them. If you are such a parent, you will be looking for ways to build an attachment with your child. You might be a parent who is simply looking for the best relationship you can have with your child. This book is rich in ideas to help you. Parents who have been through highly stressful life experiences may finally focus on their children, only to realize that they have little built in the way of positive experiences. It is not too late! Spend time playing with your children. The distance in your relationship will begin to decrease very quickly.

In healthy attachment relationships, attachments provide for emotional and physical safety for children. Attachments not only draw our children to us, but in turn, they connect us to our children. Our attachments propel us, as parents, to want to care for our children—whether or not it is convenient or comfortable. Our attachments help us to track the thoughts and feelings of those to whom we are attached. We can "feel" the thoughts and feelings of our children intensely. For example, when our children are hurt or lonely, our empathy is heightened so much that we feel a degree of their discomfort and want to alleviate it. Playing with our children is a great way to build that moment-to-moment sensitivity so that we are better at understanding how to care for our children's needs.

SECURITY IN ATTACHMENT

Attachments can come in patterns of behavior and feelings. The healthy pattern is called a "secure" attachment, since it best provides children with a sense of security. Children know that they can count on their parents. If you have a secure attachment with your children, then they trust that you will:

- keep them safe

- react sensitively to their needs

- take care of them physically and emotionally

- be reasonably available to them, while respecting your own needs

- keep your own moods and actions stable (not frightening them or being frightened yourself, except in rare emergencies)

- calm them when they are upset

- teach them to enjoy others and themselves in relationships

- encourage them to explore their worlds with joy.

In secure attachments, parents create a helpful and safe "home base." Our children can confidently leave the home base to make friends and master skills—retreating to parents for help, nurture, and recharging. The home base is not only a place of safety and nurture; parents do best to make it a place of enjoyment and fun. After all, we do not want our children to think that homes are static, boring spots that they must leave in order to enjoy themselves. This would not bode well for teen years or later adult family life.

Secure attachments have been studied by many researchers. Children with this type of attachment pattern with their parents tend to be more confident, understand the thoughts and feelings of others, as well as their own, are more resilient, respect rules and teachers, work well in groups, and are more resilient when faced with challenges. These children become adults who find it natural to form secure attachments with their own children.

There are other patterns of attachment that parents and children may form. These are patterns of *insecure* attachment. In these patterns, parents may be one or more of the following: anxious, harsh, shaming, insensitive, intrusive, rigid, cold, unstable or frightening in their moods, absent too much from their children, abusive emotionally and/or physically. In response, the children tend to show various reactions. They include children's understandable patterns of controlling parents, avoiding parents, responding anxiously to parents, and interpreting negatively the parents' intent or motives. (These attachment patterns, along with methods to move into secure attachments, are described in my books *Attaching through Love, Hugs, and Play: Simple Strategies to Help Build Connections with Your Child*; *Nurturing Adoptions: Creating Resilience after Neglect and Trauma*; and *Attaching in Adoption: Practical Tools for Today's Parents*. Please see the bibliography for more detail.)

Some parents realize that they have the ability to form secure attachments, but are parenting children who have formed one of the other patterns of attachment. This could be due to foster care or adoption, custody issues, or because of a parent's experiences with depression or addictions earlier in their child's life. Children may push away, choose strangers for closeness, resist or complain about parents' efforts to meet their children's needs, or show fear of parents when parents attempt to get close.

Parents might find that their children are set on a goal of controlling most of the parent–child time together. It can be difficult, under these circumstances, to enjoy time with your child. The rub is that often these children are open to forming superficial bonds with others while rebuffing their parents. It can feel natural to respond to children in kind—they push away, and you push away further. They control, and you become more strict and controlling. Children are negative, using their facial expressions or voices in saying "you are not doing it right." You may find yourself becoming critical in turn. As one parent said in a session with a seven-year-old in my office: "We are not having a good time. And buddy, the problem is not me!" Of course, this further solidified the pattern of control in the child, as both parent and child struggled not to feel emotionally inadequate.

When children show other patterns of attachment to parents, it can be difficult to sustain the enthusiasm necessary to move into patterns of security. The good news is that play is one of the easiest ways to break out of a negative cycle of interaction. Play tends to draw out reluctant children. It is so "in the moment" that parents find that they can relax and stop thinking of the hurt of former interactions. It is a wonderful way to share delight in each other's presence—which transforms stuck relationships.

PLEASURE, PRESSURES, PLAY, AND ATTACHMENTS

Most of the elements truly important to human survival are strongly linked with pleasure. For example, eating and sharing food are pleasurable. Adult couple relationships include sexual pleasure. Bonds between parents and children and their brothers and sisters best thrive with ample amounts of pleasure and fun in being together.

When things start to get tense in the home, parents often decide to talk more and play less. After all, the problems seem serious! Children who are already feeling shamed rarely respond better to more discussion of what is not going well. Instead, they tend to gravitate more to pleasure and fun. The fun parent who starts spending some time playing every day is much more likely to succeed in transforming their relationship than the more somber parent. Play causes children to drop their defences, and parents to drop their worries—a great combination.

Parents today are pressured by our society's expectation that their children perform. The message is "Meet standards and measure up!" In fact, many parents are in tough job or economic situations. Understandably, parents err towards spending time on family security in the form of a well-paying job, home in a safe neighborhood, and high performance—both their own at work and their children's in school. They work hard to achieve in order to maintain a stable living situation. It is common for parents to maintain non-stop access to their job through their smart phones, even if it interferes with their family time.

Playing with children may feel like a frill—something to be omitted due to the serious nature of daily life. *Instead, it is a gift that parents and children share.* It is not only wired into children to enjoy play with parents, but it is a necessary part of their development— and it is a great balance, offsetting the day-to-day pressures that parents carry. It can feel so freeing to step outside of the busyness of life to enjoy the timeless, free-flowing experiences of playing with our children.

In play children naturally have skin-to-skin contact with parents, eye contact, and a connection to the parent's body rhythms—and vice versa. Play increases children's excitement levels—and their parents' at the same time! All of these are rich in building attachments. Play causes pleasure for both parents and children—and play teaches a back-and-forth volley of enjoyment, ideas, and turns that keep both play partners happy and interested.

Play becomes one of the most important ways that we have to build bonds of attachment to our children. It helps them learn how to exist in an imaginative, mutually enjoyable space with another person. In play, children have to get on the same wavelength as the other person in order to interpret and enjoy the play. This understanding of the reciprocity, or the back-and forth nature of play will benefit children as they enter relationships with other children and teens.

Attachments, because they are so basic to children's well-being and happiness, can seem like one more task that parents have to achieve. But attachments, while crucially important to emotional and even cognitive development, are not amenable to "work-oriented" performance criteria. While basic care for children does contribute to secure attachment, there are relational aspects that are about far more than meeting basic needs. We have to have our minds and feelings available and open to our children. We cannot "do" attachment from a checklist, with our emotions and thoughts elsewhere (television, work, other tasks, our parents' faults, for example). Although we can certainly plan time for play and building our attachments, the more relational aspects of our attachments are emotional. We have to think less of our "to-do" list with our children. We shift to "being" available to our children, emotionally and physically, in order to make ourselves open to attachments. As a parent, of course you want to have a close relationship with your child. Since we are dealing with children, our closeness should include joyful, belly-laughing play times with our children.

Many parent readers will find themselves thinking, "Well, that is fine for you, but no one really played with me except in organized sports teams. I really do not have many ideas beyond a tickling game!" Other parents might say, "I'd love to play with my child if she were open to it. But she was neglected prior to our adoption. She does not seem to know how to play. When I ask her to play, she turns away." The games in this book are written for you so that you have ways to draw your children into play. Persisting positively is a skill of successful parents.

SECURE ATTACHMENTS—STRONG, KIND, PLAYFUL PARENTS AND CONFIDENT KIDS

When parents are sensitive parents, they are not marshmallows, only creating a warm lap and saying "yes." They also teach and enforce limits. They teach their children to respect the feelings and boundaries of others—parallel to how their children's thoughts and feelings are respected. There are consequences if limits are ignored. The issues of control and limits are not the main subject of this book, having been covered in depth in my books *Attaching through Love, Hugs, and Play* and *Nurturing Adoptions*. (Please see Resource List.)

Most of the time parents with secure attachments describe feeling "in sync" with their children. Children can determine where limits are by caring about their parents and understanding how stepping past limits would make their parents feel. For example, when a pre-teen's friends began to go past limits, using her mother's hat as a prop as they were playing, the girl said, "Stop. My mother loves that hat! Put it back before it gets messed up." She was laughing at her friends' antics, but persisted in getting the hat back to its spot in the closet. That is typical of children as they move through school-age years. They observe limits because they understand the underlying values of respect for the rights and belongings of others. In secure attachments, children feel "seen," significant, and know that their feelings and property are respected. This makes it easy to give such respect to others.

Secure attachments are the ideal for children's development— emotional, cognitive, and moral. Beyond the developmental influence, children/teens and parents with these attachments seem to be having such a good time for most of the childhood years! The children seem to have a confidence to them. They know that they have help if they need it, but that they can rely on themselves to figure out lots of problems in the world. Children with secure attachments tend to have high emotional intelligence. That is, they can understand the thoughts and feelings of others, as well as their own thoughts and feelings. After all, they have been practicing using these skills in their daily lives with their parents.

CREATING PATTERNS OF SECURITY AFTER ROCKY EARLY YEARS

Many parents reading this book will be forming attachments with children who have attachments that are insecure. Your children may have had high-stress beginning years—in different homes and with different parents, in many cases. The insecure attachments, instead of being marked by trust, mutual enjoyment, and a sense of being "seen" (sensitively noticed and cared for), are attachments in which children did not know whether they would be held or hurt. They may have had parents who were traumatized, which created a sense of insecurity in their children, who were aware of their parents' fearful state. Their parents may have been traumatizing, frightening their children with abuse or exposure to domestic violence. The parents may not have been able to provide even basic food and shelter consistently. Perhaps you or a previous parent figure suffered from depression, anxiety, or drug addiction. You simply were not emotionally or even physically dependable. Your child is very likely trying to control you, because they have learned that parents are unpredictable and need to be controlled. Obviously, you will want to enjoy a different pattern with your child than a tiresome one of dueling control battles. The games in this book are a way to bring your children closer to you in a more joyful manner.

There are good books written about the importance of meeting children's needs for attachment connection, including mine mentioned earlier that address children's needs at various ages/ stages of development, or under certain special conditions. This book supplements materials by providing parents with a source book that they can use to connect with their children through play.

WIRED THROUGH OUR ATTACHMENTS

Beyond basic survival, we have found that within attachment relationships, children are learning to follow the brain patterns of their parents. Without getting overly technical, researchers have found that children's brain patterns begin to mimic the brain patterns of their attachment figures—usually their parents. As parents get close to stressed or unhappy children and soothe them, children are learning to follow the soothing, calming patterns of their parents' brains. They also follow the parents' day-to-day patterns of becoming stressed and then calming themselves— hopefully, without becoming out-of-control. The degree to which children become stressed and then calm down after stress is largely a reflection of whether they are enjoying a close, secure attachment—or not. Children who are in secure attachments tend to calm down more easily after stress, and they are better at getting help and support during stressful situations.

Basically, we find that children are "borrowing" from their parents' brains. That is, they get into connection with the balanced brain patterns of their parents. They "sync up" with the stable brain patterns that their parents enjoy. This is good news for most parents whose daily patterns are ones of stable functioning. By contrast, other children have been in previous homes in which they became unbalanced by getting into connection with their parents' feelings and unstable brain patterns. These children definitely do not want to get too close to a parent again. After all, who would want to feel even more disoriented or confused?

When parents are trying to form attachments after children have had experiences like the ones above, it can be a hard sell to entice children to enjoy closeness rather than engage in control battles. Play is a lovely way to work around some of the obstacles. Play is one of the most under-utilized methods of forming attachment.

ATTACHMENT AND UNDERSTANDING HOW PEOPLE THINK (THEORY OF MIND)

When we are emotionally close to people, we open ourselves up to feeling their feelings and understanding how they think. This understanding of how the mind of another person works is called "theory of mind." In other words, we have a working model for what is important to them and what will make them upset or happy. We are connected to the extent that we know when they are getting overwhelmed—and often have a good guess of "why" they are reacting a particular way. This ability is routinely underdeveloped for children who have spent time in international orphanages or rotating foster homes. As parents play the games in this book, it will be helpful if they insert a sentence or two to encourage the growth of theory of mind. These sentences include information about how parents are feeling, or felt, playing the game with their child. Parents can briefly describe other activities that they enjoy that are similar to the game. They can note why they enjoy those activities. This helps children to develop a theory of mind about another person. Parents can basically teach their children to get to know their parents better—as well as learning how others think and feel similarly or differently. These discussions can be sprinkled throughout the play activities in this book—especially as children move into the pre-school stages and beyond.

Theory of mind is important to all of us in our day-to-day relationships. It helps us to move in unity with others—without losing our individuality. When we understand the thoughts and feelings of others we do a better job at forming close friendships, becoming positive community members, or satisfying family members. We spend less time apologizing for insensitive actions, since we typically negotiate life with an awareness of how others are likely to think or feel in work or home situations.

Often we learn about sensitivity through the negative side. People point out to us when we err. For children who have a background that is filled with shame, this is a bruising teaching method. An easier way to expand a person's abilities in this area is through play. Children learn to negotiate play experiences when they have not erred in any way. Instead, they are learning in a fun-filled, creative, or high excitement experience. All it takes is a few sentences within the play time about how parents are feeling during the game, and what their thoughts and motivations are. For example, in the "airplane ride" game, the parent can say, "I love holding you close like this. It makes me happy. I wonder which is more fun for us—to swing you out fast like this [demonstrate]—or to go two times slowly [demonstrate again]?" In the choices, you, the parent, are accompanying the emotional information with your actions. You can ask your child to look at your face and guess which is your favorite, and ask your child to guess why you like the game. (You can provide the answers a few moments before so that your child is able to guess correctly.) Of course, great answers are that you like being with your child, or laughing, or having fun! The balance in incorporating some theory of mind is to keep the game spontaneous fun, but still include some insight-developing words here and there. The activity does not turn into a teaching exercise, but does include some teaching moments.

EMOTIONAL "SKILLS" AND ATTACHMENT

Overlapping the discussion of "theory of mind" above, secure attachments help children to develop skills to cope with and understand daily life. Within the relationships with their parents, children's brains are forming the abilities to put things in perspective, calm, understand the point of view of another, understand the feelings of another, be aware of their own thoughts and feelings, stand up for themselves, and build frustration tolerance. These skills fall under a loose heading of "*executive functions.*" The degree to which our children will feel successful has a lot to do with the development of these abilities. While the presence or absence of these abilities is partly genetic, the abilities can be shaped for the better with input from parents who are forming and maintaining secure attachments.

This book invites parents to do two seemingly contradictory things at once. On the one hand, parents are being asked to pay close attention to creating secure attachments (bonds) with their children; those close connections are critical to the way our children develop long-term emotional well-being. On the other hand, parents are asked to be less serious about their relationships—and play more!

In the next chapter we will further explore the value of play in children's development.

Chapter 2

The Value of Play

MEGAN CLARKE

It is a happy talent to know how to play.

Ralph Waldo Emerson

What does it mean to play? Our adult lives are filled with work, school functions, soccer games, bills to pay—grown-up activities. Sometimes it feels like we rarely have the time to play. What does play really mean? We know it is great for children, especially for our children with insecure attachments—but not as important for us, right? In the last chapter we talked about how play can deepen attachment with our children and create deeper bonds between siblings and within families. In this chapter we will explore the importance of play for adults and children and look at it within the context of our society and our health.

Today's world is busy. We have competing priorities pulling at us at all times. Our achievement-focused society drives families to focus on multiple activities at once. As adults, we balance career, family, financial success, spiritual involvement, and community service. Society views play as part of childhood and not a worthy activity for adults. An adult who indulges in fun, frivolous activities can be viewed as irresponsible or not serious; it is kids' stuff. Children today spend tremendous time on academic achievement, music lessons, sports, and art. The constant drive to achieve requires us to focus our intentions and efforts into other's expectations.

Science is beginning to challenge this notion that play is extraneous. Research is uncovering not only the benefit, but the need, of play for our overall health. Play improves a sense of belonging, emotional connection and quality of work. Companies like Google incorporate a sense of playfulness in their work environments because they believe it fosters creativity and innovation. We can gain a greater sense of overall happiness and satisfaction with our lives when we incorporate play as individuals, couples and families.

PLAY DEFINED

When we talk about play, what do we mean? Is it just board games, tag, or baseball? In his book, *Play: How It Shapes the Brain, Opens the Imagination, and Invigorates the Soul*, Stuart Brown describes play not as a specific activity but more as a state of mind. Stuart defines play as: "an absorbing, apparently purposeless activity that provides enjoyment and a suspension of self-consciousness and sense of time."[1] He contends that it is self-motivating and makes you want to do the activity again. Viewing play from within this framework opens up the options of what we can consider play, but also individualizes it. While one person may find card games enjoyable, another may lose themselves in painting a landscape. Cooking an elaborate meal may engage one person, while hitting the trails for a long run may appeal to another. Play can be an individual activity or shared together. It can be adventuresome or tucked away at home. Viewing play in this way opens endless options for enjoyment that can enrich our lives.

PLAY AND YOUR CHILD'S DEVELOPMENT

Not only is play enjoyable and exciting for children; it helps them develop many aspects of their emerging selves. When you watch a child create an imaginary world, manipulate a squishy ball or

1   Brown, S. (2009) *Play: How it Shapes the Brain, Opens the Imagination, and Invigorates the Soul.* New York: Penguin Group. p.60.

compete in a baseball game, many exiting changes are taking place in their concept of themselves and in their ways of understanding the world.

As we spend time engaged in one-on-one play with our children, we focus our attention and interest in their actions and reactions. We laugh when they do something funny and we celebrate as they complete a task successfully. This undivided attention contributes greatly to their sense of self-worth. As we delight in them, children internalize the message that they are wonderful, interesting, and important. You can see this as children try to become even sillier or sing a little louder to receive more attention. This selective attention to the positive proves to be especially beneficial for children with early trauma and who may have learned to gain attention through negative behaviors. The joy they feel from our attention to their play is reinforcing; they want more of that wonderful attention! Children can learn to obtain attention for being positive or endearing rather than negative. Our interaction with them fills their little bodies with positive emotions and helps them understand how wonderful they really are. What a gift to all children!

Creating a fantasy world or wonderful stories helps children to learn to use their imagination. Early in childhood, imaginative play helps children learn to create a narrative, with beginning, middle and end, all of which begins to develop the ability to organize their life stories. As they grow, using their imagination, children constantly move back and forth between reality and fantasy, trying on different personalities. A well-developed imaginative life has been linked to emotional resilience and creativity throughout life.

Play also develops a positive sense of self-esteem, which is so important in a child's life. Think of a child working on a puzzle with an adult. As she approaches this new task, she stretches her learning skills. She must work diligently to find the pieces, trying different shapes and strategies, while potentially experiencing frustration. The parent encourages and helps offer tips or ideas. Over time, the child learns to tolerate the negative emotion and persevere. When the puzzle is completed, she can enjoy the parent's praise and her own success. She learns that she can work hard and have success. In this simple example of a puzzle, we can see the traits of strong self-esteem developing in the child which will serve her well throughout life: diligence, creativity, innovation, frustration tolerance, mastery, and optimism. We can see this growth in all types of play, whether creating art, competing in a sport or writing a story. The experience can be rich and nourishing for your child's spirit.

Mutual play can make our world a better place in that it fosters empathy. When children play together or play with adults, they must step into another's experience. You can see this happen as children create an imaginative world or game together. Each child offers their ideas about the story, characters or rules while listening and considering the suggestions of the others. This back and forth interaction creates opportunity to understand another's point of view, experience, hopes, and desires. Depending on the ages of the children, parents are often important components in this development during the play by encouraging listening and taking turns sharing. Through multiple experiences, children develop skills in negotiation, cooperation, and fairness, all of which form the basis of friendship and empathy.

THE IMPORTANCE OF PLAY FOR PARENTS

As you will see in the way the following chapters are organized, play can improve attachment between parents and children, siblings, and whole families. The benefits of play extend throughout our adult lives as well. Play improves our sense of belonging. When we engage in playful activities, we tap into our emotions and thoughts and then share them with others. When we watch our favorite TV show or view an art exhibit and then discuss it with others, we increase a sense of community and connection. Think of the camaraderie when cities cheer on their favorite sports team to victory. Sharing a passion of collecting antiques with others allows discussion of our interests and what we value. Our sense of belonging to something bigger than ourselves expands when we share in such activities.

Play improves emotional connections between participants. In order to engage someone else in a playful activity, we need to open ourselves up to them and invite mutual connections. You can't truly enjoy a playful activity if your defenses are up and you are closed off. Play requires us to interact with the outside world while expressing our needs and desires. Creating and sharing our art requires an opening of ourselves to others and an opportunity for them to respond to us. Being silly or trying something new allows us to expose parts of our selves that we may not share when completing mundane tasks. Even joking around or teasing each other requires paying attention to the other person's response to the joke and adjusting our response as needed.

Play improves our work lives. Our achievement-driven society holds a common misconception that work and play are opposites. Play can invigorate our work, nourish creativity and foster ingenuity. When we play, we open ourselves to novelty, analyze new situations and solve puzzles. We are forced to think differently, which can be refreshing and re-energizing. After a playful vacation, people often return to work with new attitudes, ideas, and energy.

Play improves our adult lives in far-reaching ways: through improved sense of belonging, emotional connections, and more satisfying work and home life. Play should be more highly valued by our society because it makes it a better society with happier, more satisfied members.

LET'S BE PLAYFUL

We can see the benefits of play for healthy attachment and overall happiness for ourselves, children, families, and community. The remainder of this book details lovely games and activities for children of all ages. Each game details how it influences attachment, how to play, ways it can be altered, and things to think about. It is packed full of wonderful information to help parents and caregivers improve their relationship with their children.

We all want to parent well, to raise happy, loving children ready to move successfully through this complicated world. We read books and articles on parenting, listen to experts and watch others. We worry about and analyze our parenting skills and those of others. This parenting stuff is serious, tough work!

At the same time, in our discussion about play, we learn how important it is for our children's happiness as well as our own. Play should be a purposeless activity in which we lose a sense of time. We should play for the sheer enjoyment of it and of those with whom we play! There is an element of irony in compiling a book with details specifically on how to play with our children.

So, let's begin to relax and get ready to play. We know that the work of raising children, especially children with insecure attachment, can be challenging at times. Thinking about playing with a child who knows exactly which buttons to push or a child who resists positive interaction may, on certain days, feel like too much. This is where we want to encourage you to be gentle with yourself. There is no absolute right or wrong way to do these games and activities. Use your judgment and instincts. You can be flexible and adapt them to the needs of your child. If your child has been affected by drugs, alcohol or other toxins, the final chapter suggests specific adjustments which may make the games more fun.

Before you begin an activity, pay attention to moods, both yours and your child's. Is either of you tired? Hungry? Stressed by other influences? There is no need to force something that isn't right at the time. If you begin a game and there is just too much resistance, feel free to pick it up another time. For children who struggle with managing their emotions, the excitement of the game may be a lot to handle. The importance of the joyful exchange is more important than completing the task. Be mindful and follow their pacing. Trust your instincts. Remind yourself you are a good parent who wants the best for your children, and are trying hard. Now, let's begin playing.

Connecting Through Games

Chapter 3

Connecting the Two of You

Infant and toddler play

When forming attachments with infants and toddlers, we emphasize activities that are rich in potential for attachment formation. Examples include: eye contact and gaze, skin-to-skin contact or touching, motions that include swinging, movements that cause our children to reach out to cling to us, shared emotion or laughing together, voice rhythms that move in pitch and intensity from soothing to excited, and back-and-forth turn-taking that includes some surprises and delight.

Playing with little ones is sensation-rich. Creating different feelings in their bodies with movement, heightening emotions that both parents and children are feeling, surprising them with a novel facial expression—all these are the silly and enjoyable ways that we build connection. As we play, our little ones experience us as uniquely interesting. Through play we help them to build a self-concept of being interesting and worth our time.

Most of the games or activities at this stage are highly physical. Parents are on the floor with children, touching, holding, swinging, and even blowing on little bellies. We recognize how essential we are to our children—the center of their worlds at this stage. We are teaching them that close connections are enjoyable and fun.

Some of the games in this section will work not only for this stage, but through several years into the future. They are placed in this section so that they are easy to find.

AIRPLANE RIDE

Contributed by Deborah Gray

Age: 18 months to 5 years

Play time: 1–5 minutes

Airplane rides help little people to connect with their parents. When parents pick up children, the movement stimulates high excitement in children—and in parents. Flying through the air lets our children relax control and trust us as they experience the delight of being airborne. Wonderfully, we share that feeling together.

How to play

Either child or parent can ask to play airplane ride. Parents ask, "Do you want to go on a ride on an airplane?" Parents can pick up their little one under the arms, twirling them in an arc around the parent's body. Parents swing around in a semicircle in order to allow the feeling of movement and some centrifugal force. As children squeal with delight, parents can repeat the play. (Don't swing children from their hands since it is too hard on their shoulder joints.)

Some children like support under their bellies as they swing, so that the parent swings in almost a complete circle, the child's trunk being supported by both of the parent's forearms. Typically children laugh loudly and ask for more and more rides. The activity works well because of the shared excitement, movement, and skin-to-skin contact that it provides. Parents and children will exchange looks, and squeaks, of delight.

Parents can elaborate on the game by asking, "Where is the airplane going?" They pick destinations, comment on how close they are, and what they are seeing. They can speed up or slow down. "Landing" can be a smooth landing or a bouncing one onto a sofa or bed.

Comments on the game

This is a super game to play on a rainy day when children and parents feel shut in. Bored, cranky children will enjoy the physical activity. It helps parents to break a low energy cycle if they feel themselves just plodding along. The parents get some much-needed exercise while the children get fun, connection, and excitement. This can also be a great game prior to dinner when parents and children have just gotten back to the home after work or pre-school. It helps set the mood for a playful and emotionally connected evening. Children who need a higher level of stimulation enjoy this activity. Parents who find themselves distracted by phones, mental lists, and the trivia of life will find this game a way to leave those distractions behind.

REVERSE SWINGING

Contributed by Deborah Gray

Age: Toddler (the child needs to be able either to grip or sit in an enclosed seat) through about 8 years (or older if the child still enjoys it)

Play time: 1–10 minutes

This activity is a variation of a time-honored childrens' favorite— swinging on swings. When our children swing, we typically push them from the rear. In this game, parents increase the attachment potential of the activity. By standing in front of your child, you are able to share facial expressions, playfully grab and tickle little feet, add a singsong about how much you love your child, and increase or decrease the speed or size of the arc by following the facial expressions of your child.

How to play

Parents help their child onto the swing, then take off the child's shoes, so that the child is in socks or bare feet. The parent pulls the child toward themselves, starting the swinging arc. They sing or chant words like, "You swing away," as their child swings away, and "You always come back," as their child swings back. Then the parent holds and tickles or strokes the soles of their little one's feet, starting the arc again.

Parents can vary how long they hold their child at the top of the arc—increasing excitement and anticipation. They can use other words that best fit their situations. As children get older, it is a natural opportunity for children to put their feelings into words. Parents can prompt children to add some verbal expression. "Is that too high? Are you afraid?" Or "Are you feeling safe and excited?"

Comments on the game

Children who have attachment anxiety really like this game. They have the closeness and connection of the parent's presence, and they are able to hear the back-and-forth message that they can swing away from the parent without "losing" them. Children like the soothing nature of the swinging, which then switches into a more exciting push. They like being able to ask for, or to anticipate, differences in speed. Since they need to communicate their wishes to parents, they increase eye contact and the verbal expressions of their feelings. For example: "Too high! I like that. I love you, Mommy. Higher, I'm not scared!" All of these are helping children to express their feelings and attune to parents.

This is an easy way to play your way towards more secure attachment with your child.

ROW, ROW, ROW YOUR BOAT

Contributed by Julie Fisher

Age: Infants/Toddlers
Play time: 1–10 minutes

Infants and toddlers, in particular, connect through music and song. The tune of "Row, row, row your boat" is well-known and very accessible for parents and children. When combined with arm and leg motions and using eye contact, this simple song becomes a powerful tool for connecting with children. It is particularly useful in moments of disconnect, or when a parent wants to intercept in a downward behavioral spiral with a toddler; and many children benefit from feeling more balance—through either increasing their energy or calming down—while playing this game.

How to play

The parent or child can suggest/request this game. They get on the floor together, facing each other, and hold hands. If the child is big enough, they also put their feet up against each other, forming a "boat." If the child is an infant or very small toddler, the parent may want the child in her lap. This is also an option for an older child who is not yet comfortable with direct eye contact; the parent and child can be facing the same direction. Gently moving back and forth in a rhythmic, see-saw motion, parent and child begin to sing: "Row, row, row your boat, gently down the stream; Merrily, merrily, merrily, merrily, life is but a dream." Then, come the next two verses, the ones children usually get very excited about: "Row, row, row your boat, gently down the stream; If you see an alligator, don't forget to SCREAM!" Oh, the thrill! The child realizes he/she is **allowed** to **scream**! And then a third verse, which is almost as exciting: "Row, row, row your boat, gently to the shore; If you see a lion, don't forget to ROAR!" Again, there is great excitement and anticipation as parent and child get ready to roar together.

Once these three verses are mastered, some optional additions are:

- "…gently down the Nile; If you see a camel, don't forget to smile";

- "…gently down the river; If you see a polar bear, don't forget to shiver";

- "…gently in the bath; If you see a tall giraffe, don't forget to laugh."

This game can be adapted to include siblings by having one sibling on the parent's lap so they are both facing the other child. It can be a fun and safe way to reconnect two squabblers after a particularly trying morning of wanting all the same toys.

Comments on the game

The key to this game, like most games with young children, is reading the child's cues accurately. Is the game bringing the child into a place of better self-regulation and connection with the parent? Does the parent genuinely enjoy the game? Are there opportunities to improvise and be silly? If the child wants to sing the "ROAR" verse over and over again, is that okay with the parent? Does the parent need to help the child calm down with "…life is but a dream" because nap time is on the horizon?

Because of the hands and feet motion, this game also provides sensory input to the players. Getting to push on a parent's feet and pull with the hands provides extra feedback about where a child is in space. This game can also be used as a ritual to signify a transition. A child may come to expect that this game is played when a visitor first comes into the home and right before he leaves. Games can help young children understand time and boundaries, and can relieve the anxiety that comes with unknowns and changes to the routine.

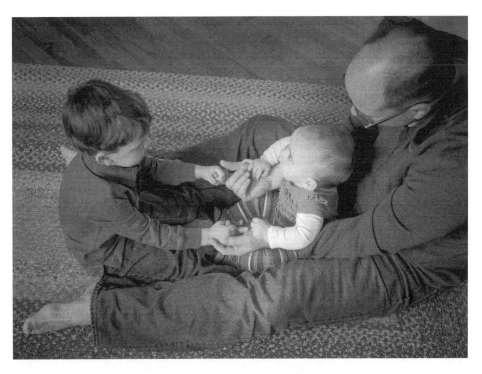

Figure 3.1: Row, row, row your boat

PIANO

Contributed by Julie Fisher

Age: Toddlers and Pre-schoolers
Play time: 2–10 minutes

This game capitalizes on novelty and unpredictability. For those who remember the television show **The Gong Show**, this game will sound familiar. The "Playing the piano" game allows for creativity, along with physical closeness and practicing balance. Depending on the strength in a parent's legs, this game is typically suitable for children under 40 pounds.

How to play

A parent can ask a child, "Do you want to play the piano?" The parent then lies down on her back and bends her knees so that her knees are a little higher than the height of the child's legs (think bike seat height). The child is then invited to sit on the parent's knees and "play" the parent's fingers that are held up and towards the child like piano keys. A pillow or cushion supporting her upper back will likely be needed to make this comfortable for the parent.

As the child "plays" the piano, she is encouraged to sing a song or hum a tune of her choosing—and/or the parent can make requests. As the child sings, the parent can decide at any time to "drop" the child by flattening her legs. (The parent will support the child so she doesn't get hurt when this happens, and will do this extremely gently the first time they are playing the game so as to not scare the child.)

As the child learns the piano game, this "drop" comes as a playful and eagerly anticipated surprise and usually brings lots of laughter. The parent jokes and says things like, "Can you sing it faster/slower/louder/ quieter?" Or "That's not 'Twinkle, Twinkle, Little Star'!" and proceeds to sing it in falsetto to the child. The idea is to connect through silliness and a physical representation of the basis of connection; the "serve and return." If the child doesn't like being dropped, she can request not to be dropped. The parent, through reading the child's reactions, varies the length of time she listens to the song and the amount of drama she puts into the moment of dropping her legs (or metaphorically "banging the gong"). The game continues until either player gets bored of it. It naturally lends itself to transitioning to other physical, on-the-floor games such as "Row, row, row your boat."

Comments on the game

When energy and connectedness are low, this is a good game for parents to try. Most children love to sing, and the novelty that a parent can *be* a piano is hard to resist. So often children who were neglected as infants didn't experience games like "peek-a-boo." This game shares that kind of "peek-a-boo" excitement because a child doesn't know when he will feel the sensation of falling, just as an infant doesn't know when a parent's face will appear from behind his hands. Each time a child connects with his parent after having this mutual moment of excitement, their attachment grows a little.

Since a parent is too big to sit on a child's legs to play a child's "piano," one way to turn this game around and shift control is to have the child stick out her fingers to be "played" by the parent, while they are both upright on their knees facing each other. If the child doesn't like the parent's song, she can withdraw her "piano keys." The parent can react with high drama and upset, saying things like, "That was my best version!" Or "Wait, you didn't hear the chorus yet!" Any way you play the piano game, giggling is a good indicator of success!

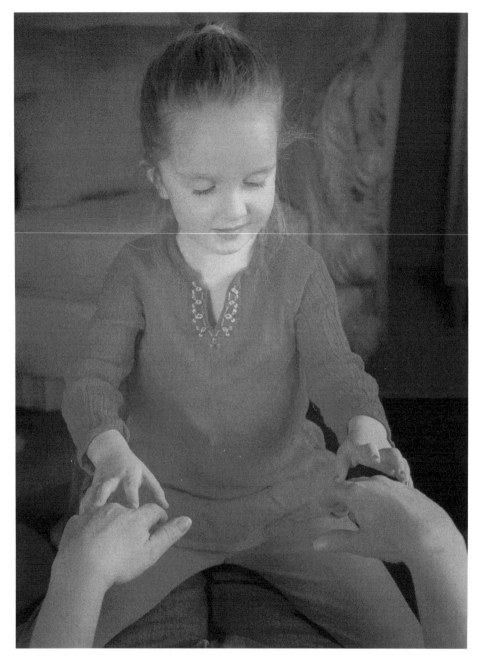

Figure 3.2: Playing the piano

THIS LITTLE PIGGY

Contributed by Julie Fisher

Age: Infants/Toddlers
Play time: 1–5 minutes

This eighteenth-century English nursery rhyme is well-known and easy to remember. It requires no equipment and takes advantage of daily nurturing activities as its playing field. Since attachment is built through nurturing and play, this game combines the two seamlessly.

How to play

Infants and toddlers are often taking their shoes off, wanting to go barefoot, or they are barefoot because it is time for a diaper change or a bath. This game gives the parent a context for adoring those cute little "piggies" on a child's feet through play. A parent will grab the big toe and say, "This little piggy went to the market!" Then, the next toe: "This little piggy stayed home." The middle toe: "This little piggy had roast beef." The fourth toe: "This little piggy had none!" And finally, the last little ("pinky") toe: "This little piggy cried 'wee, wee, wee,' all the way home!" At this point, the parent can tickle the feet and/or tickle up the child's arm towards his chin for "all the way home."

A parent can add new verses, tones, or even do this game to her own toes or invite the child to join in and be more comfortable. This game has the climax of the "wee, wee, wee" part that gets parents and children giggling, but it also provides a nice pathway for a parent to transition to a foot massage with her young child. We know that attachment is enhanced through the soothing that comes from touching the soles of a child's feet.[2] This game gets there naturally and playfully.

---

2   Gray, D. D. (2014) *Attaching Through Love, Hugs, and Play*. London: Jessica Kingsley Publishers. p.33.

Comments on the game

Everyone loves ritual, but infants and toddlers bask in it. This game has been passed down from generation to generation because it employs ritual. It becomes "that thing you do" together. It is playful. After a child learns this game, she may thrust her toes at you and request it at any and all future opportunities.

This game also gives an easy "pet" name to the child's toes: the "Pigs" or the "Piggies." There is a natural chance to practice boundaries and limits in this game. A parent can show a child she understands "no" and less subtle cues, if this game is not what the child had in mind. It can also be gradual. Perhaps the story ends with the piggy being at the market. Perhaps it develops from there, child-led, into telling what things the family buys when at the "market." There is not a "wrong" way to play this game; if it is bringing about connection, then it is working.

Finally, it is very simple for an older sibling to join in, particularly after you have modeled the ways the game tends to be best received. Sometimes, having this "excuse" (for playing with a younger sibling) allows an older child to go back and enjoy a younger way to connect that he hasn't experienced for a long time. In the case of children who have been abused or neglected, this "going back" may be their first experience of "baby games." You can jump in and normalize that *everyone* has piggies and they all "go to market" on occasion.

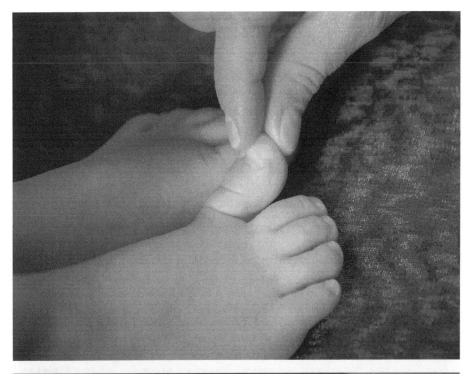

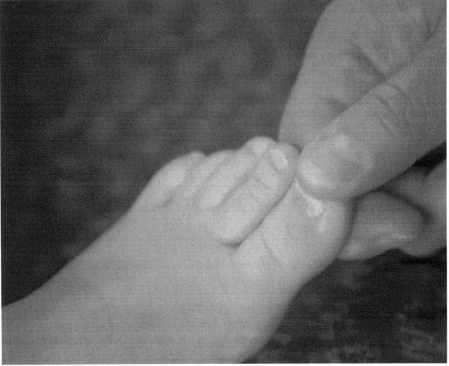

Figure 3.3: This little piggy

PONY BOY/GIRL

Contributed by Deborah Gray

Age: Toddler through about 7 years (depending on build of child and parent)

Play time: 1–10 minutes

This was a favorite game of my children. "Pony boy" or "Pony girl" is a song that pairs well with the knee bouncing that is part of the game. The song is from a folk song. (Parents who do not know the tune can reference YouTube or Bruce Springsteen's version, which are on the internet.) The song and "ride" (your child bouncing on your knees) are fun, can vary in speed and bounce height, and include lots of opportunities for hugs and shared, positive expressions. We changed the gender of the song's pony randomly.

How to play

Parents sit on a low couch or chairs. Sit with your legs sticking out. The child climbs on your knees for a "ride." As the parent sings, the legs bounce in rhythm. Once the rider is comfortable, the child can ask for fast or slow. I would use a lot of trembling within the bounces, or lower children between the knees and almost to the floor in order to increase the excitement of the game. (Of course, I was careful not to drop them.) Part of the fun is the variation in the game, along with ample opportunities for hugs and squeals of laughter.

Sometimes I fit two children on my knees, with both children hanging on and giggling. I once attempted three children. However, that required a little more strength and leg room than I had. My husband did have three at a time, all of whom asked for repeats!

Comments on the game

If you have children who seek out physical play and who like rough-and-tumble play, then this game can be a great one for them. It can be rowdy and physical. While it encourages close body contact, it still has the predictability provided by the length of the song. That will help kids who tend to get overstimulated. They can downplay their excitement as you approach the end of the song.

If you have a more cautious child, the activity can as easily be altered to be soothing, with steady rhythm and a reduced, reliant bounce. The "pony boy" song can be sung as more of a lullaby for the child who likes a narrower band of stimulation.

What I like best about this activity is that it ends with parents and children leaning into the finale of a big hug.

Figure 3.4: Pony boy/girl

AGE 3 AND UP

Attaching to children in the three years and older group includes the sensory-rich activities that are in the infant/toddler games. We have opportunity to add more language and "what if" themes, since children's vocabularies and imagination are expanding rapidly. Those qualities allow the opportunity for a more complex exchange of ideas. It gives children the chance to hear about, reflect on, and contribute to relationships. We want to give children the chance to shape our play, so that it reflects their growing sense of mastery. Do not be surprised if little ones are bossy right through ages four or five. This is a normal part of their development. Rather than acting offended, do incorporate their bossiness into the play, perhaps exaggerating it a little and responding in a playful manner.

In the games in this section, it becomes more obvious that parents are using their attachment relationship to learn about the other's preferences—which builds the child's emotional intelligence. Parents are promoting the development of theory of mind, as described in Chapter 1, as well as teaching children how to get in tune with their parents. Happily, this is done in the most pleasant manner through these games.

Often children in this stage of development are playing with a purpose. They will bring ideas into the play that are typical fears and dreams of children of their age. Examples of these are superhero powers, concerns about dying or being lost, or ideas about being endowed with great powers, talents, strength, or loveliness. They will also include information about things that may have caused them loss or pain in the past. Often they will play out fighting people who are or were hurtful, and having you, as parents, join in to help them. If children move from the games into some of this imaginative play, it helps them to feel a sense of mastery. They can enjoy the parent's support as parents allow them to express their emotions during the play.

Themes that parents want to bring out during any play or games are ones that include parents being strong, nurturing, and kind to their children, as well as capable of keeping their children safe. This is an age in which magic flourishes. Parents who incorporate themes of flying, talking animals, other worlds, and great adventures, can spice up the play time without sacrificing the ideal of their children living in a predictable and secure world. Parents can simply "land" their children back onto their own street and home at the end of the adventure.

MUSICAL CHAIRS

Contributed by Laura Stone

Age: 3–7

Play time: 3–5 minutes

Traditionally, the game of "musical chairs" often leads to someone feeling left out, as there are more children than chairs, and players are eliminated one by one as the chairs decrease with each turn. In this take on the familiar game, the parent invites the child to use his or her lap as the "chair." Rather than being left out, children are brought closer by being sung to and cuddled in the parent's lap in a fun way. Young children delight in being claimed by their parents, and this game offers an opportunity for the child first to hear their parent sing to them and about them, and then to be claimed with a hug when the music stops. For children who are connecting with new parents, this activity offers an exciting but low-pressure way to play and experience nurturing touch and words.

How to play

Find an area free of furniture or other obstacles, where the child can safely run in a circle around the parent. The parent sits on floor or ground, and the child stands up. The parent begins to sing a made-up song about the child or about the two of them together, "Oh, today is a special day… [child's name] and Mommy are here to play," etc., while the child walks or runs in a circle around the parent. The parent may sing softly and slowly, or speed up the song and increase the volume, and then slow down and sing softly again—some suspense adds to the fun. When the parent stops singing, the child is to find the parent's lap as quickly as possible. The parent hugs the child, and both are likely to giggle. The parent might say, "Oh, I'm so glad you are here! I was really hoping you would find my lap because I love to hold you!" The parent can expect requests from the child to do it again.

Comments on the game

This is a great game to play when parents or children are feeling a little disconnected or unfocused, such as upon waking from a nap or coming together again after spending time apart. The movement, melody and physical connection will ease tension and refocus parent and child.

Some young children are very sensitive to touch and will need to be hugged gently, while others have a tendency to use too much force; this game also offers an opportunity to practice coming together in a way that feels right for both. For a child who is sensitive to touch, the hugging part of the game provides an opportunity to find just the right amount of pressure that feels good, and for the child who has a tendency to slam into others, parents can help them practice sitting down quickly but gently in the parent's lap when the music stops.

SONGS ABOUT US

Contributed by Laura Stone

Age: 3–5
Play time: 3–5 minutes

Most children delight in hearing their parents sing about them. Newly adopted young children often need help to understand how they are connected to their new parent(s), and special songs that connect "mommy" or "daddy" and the child's name in the lyrics can be a simple but powerful way to develop a sense of belonging together.

How to play

This activity will be most effective if the child and parent make eye contact and comfortable physical contact while singing. The child, facing the parent, may be seated either in the parent's lap, or on the parent's outstretched legs. The parent starts a song that connects the two of them, using a familiar tune. For example, to the tune of "Oh, Susanna:" "Oh, my mama, she's the one for me; Well, we're eatin' a banana with my blankie on my knee." Or "Oh, my [child's name], he's the one for me; Well, we're here right now together, just my [child's name] and me." Add movements, such as gentle bouncing or gentle clapping, if desired.

If your child, especially your newly adopted child, turns away or wants you to stop singing, take a break and try again another time, but keep trying. Make sure songs are upbeat and happy, not forlorn. For example, avoid such lyrics as "Please don't take my sunshine away," as these can cause anxiety and detract from building connections. Make up several songs and pay attention to which ones the child most enjoys. Sing often. Use the favorite song to help your child calm in times of distress. Have fun.

Comments on the game

Whether children are in the first weeks of being at home, or whether they have been in the family a long time, this activity offers an easy and soothing way to affirm the parent–child relationship. Parents might sing the favorite song to children in the car on an outing, to reinforce their connection prior to being in a situation with many people, or perhaps as part of a bedtime ritual to soothe nighttime fears. Over time, children will remember these songs and can use them to soothe themselves during time away from parents.

PAPER PEOPLE

Contributed by Deborah Gray

Age: 3–5
Play time: 20–60 minutes

When we are looking for attachment and bonding activities to do with children, this is one of the best! Making paper people helps us to project our feelings onto the figures. It allows us to express just what we wish to our children, as we use figures to represent the two of us. Best of all, this project can be saved and adapted so that the paper people can be posed differently on another day.

How to make this project

You will need to get large rolls of shelf paper or large sheets from a craft store. (You may have to tape a few large pieces of heavy paper together.) Unroll the paper onto a clean, smooth floor. Have your child lie down on the paper. Then, draw around your child. By itself, this part of the process is fun. (Do not follow the inseam of the pants the entire way to the crotch, which would be a little creepy. Make a detour a few inches below the crotch, moving over to the other leg.) Next, have your child draw their hair, eyes, and mouth with crayons or markers, and with your help as needed. (Almost all children like to have a smile on their faces.) Cut out the paper person that will be your "paper child."

Next, put large paper down for yourself. Draw around yourself with your child's help. This is almost always a funny experience, with some giggling as you try to reach around yourself with your child's help.

You and your child can draw on your features and smiling face. Then cut yourself out. Pose the child and parent together. Follow the child's lead with ideas of whether you should pose the child as getting a hug from the parent, being held, or holding hands. Because the paper people are representing you and your child, you are able to insert some strong and positive emotional messages. The paper arms of the parent can embrace the child, for example. When you like the poses, tape the paper people to a surface that you and your child can see. Some children like these on the bedroom walls to see when they wake up.

The people can be moved to other poses when children are ready. For example, a book could be drawn and taped in for the paper parent to read to the paper child; or ice cream cones could be drawn and placed so that both paper child and paper parent enjoy a treat together. (Feel free to take the suggestions in real life.)

Comments on the activity

This is a wonderful way to express to children how you feel about them. By working on this project children are able to give feelings to the "paper people" as well as connect to their own feelings. It is a lovely way to help children understand secure attachments. As paper parents smile down at children from walls, they are silent witnesses to the power of love. These "paper people" may be rolled up to be saved in your keepsake boxes.

OTHER ACTIVITIES

Contributed by Laura Stone

Age: 3–5
Play time: 3–5 minutes

Here is a short list of simple activities children and their parents can do together:

Handprints: Create handprints in paint. The parent can make his or her handprint on paper by first dipping the hand in a light-colored paint. When the parent's handprint is slightly dry, have the child make his or her handprint in a darker paint color on top and inside the shape of the parent's handprint.

Nose touches: Make a game of touching noses with your young child. Take care not to bang heads together in the process.

Blow bubbles: Blow through straws into a bowl of soapy water together. It works great.

Homemade playdough: Fun recipes are widely available online—fun to make and fun to play with together.

Watch bugs: Find some ants outside and see what they do.

Face paint: Make sure to use non-toxic materials.

Hairdresser: Make a game of brushing and styling each other's hair.

Look at clouds: Lie in the grass and look up. Describe what you see to each other.

Macaroni necklace: Make some jewelry from noodles or ring-shaped cereal. Wear each other's creations.

Roll a ball: For active kids, try rolling or gently bouncing a ball back and forth while you talk. It may make it easier to focus and stay engaged.

Go swimming: Getting in the water together can be both stimulating and relaxing. Help your child learn to float on their back and relax, while you support them. Gently move them around in the water with your hands under their back and neck.

Selfies: Use your phone or camera to take silly pictures of the two of you, photobooth style. Giggle while you look at them together.

MAKE A MURAL

Contributed by Deborah Gray

Age: 5 and up
Play time: 20–60 minutes

It is wonderful to capture and reflect on the positives in our families and homes. This activity helps us to do just that with our children. In making a mural, we usually pick out a certain time frame or event that we want our children to notice and celebrate with us. The making of the mural allows children to reflect on positives and to store those memories.

How to make this project

You will need to get large rolls of shelf paper or large sheets from a craft store. You can roll out the paper onto a long table, temporarily securing it with masking tape. You and your child will want to talk about the mural and what goes on it. Getting ready for grandparents' or cousins' visit might be a theme. Another could be "Our camping trip."

The child or children will each have an area of the mural. They can draw the part that they most want to remember. If they want to, they can use pictures from magazines to help with their space. Most children enjoy drawing their own ideas, but will often ask for technical assistance. If someone gets frustrated and scribbles out a section of their mural, tape in a "do-over" patch. It is a nice example of family life.

Whether the mural is worked on for several days, or just one, depends on the project and how much children are enjoying it. When it is done, it is taped rather low (child's eye level) along a kitchen, living room or hall wall. It just depends how much space is available. The parents' part is to draw themselves into areas of the mural, as a smiling face enjoying their children's activities, or also preparing for the mural's event.

Comments on the activity

Reflecting on shared good times, or events to which we are looking forward, helps us all to see our families positively. We store our memories in a way that makes us value our families. This is a tool to help our children to feel connected and part of a positive whole. Your child will feel proud of her work, and will show the parts of the mural that make her happiest. At the same time, she will see that she is an important part of a family in which people are enjoying doing things together.

BACK DRAWINGS

Contributed by Laura Stone

Age: 5 and up
Play time: 5–10 minutes

Children need safe and nurturing touch. Regular gentle touch from parents can help children pay attention better, sleep better and longer, stay emotionally regulated (balanced) longer, lower stress hormones in the body, and improve overall health and functioning. Children also benefit from their parents' loving words, in terms of maintaining self-esteem and positive self-image, internalizing a sense of emotional safety, developing empathy, and building relational skills. Sometimes kids absorb these parental strokes and messages better when they come somewhat indirectly. This activity provides an opportunity for parents to give nurturing touch and non-verbal positive messages to their child in a way that is fun and relaxed.

How to play

The parent sits on the floor or ground, criss-cross (cross-legged) or comfortable with legs apart and outstretched. The child sits in front of the parent with his or her back to the parent, so the child's back is touching the parent's knees. The child has a pad of plain paper and a marker in their lap. The parent draws a picture on the child's back using a pointer finger. Draw something simple to start—maybe a smiley face. The child draws the same image on the paper using his or her sense of touch to interpret what the parent has drawn. The parent can increase the complexity of the drawings gradually, or keep it simple. Words or symbols can also be written—think of drawing an eye, then a heart, then the letter "U." Children may want a turn to draw on Mom or Dad's back as well.

Comments on the game

Most kids are curious and will be intrigued by this activity, wanting to decipher what the parent has drawn. Through the action of redrawing what the parent creates, the child may integrate the *message* more deeply.

This game could easily be expanded to include more family members, as in "Telephone," with the family seated in a loose circle, facing front to back, with one family member holding the paper in his or her lap. The parent draws the original image on the back of the family member in front of them, the next person draws on the back in front of them, and so on, until the last person is left to draw on the paper. It is fun to see how close or different the final interpretation is to the original!

SCRIBBLE

Contributed by Laura Stone

Age: 5 and up

Play time: 5–10 minutes

D.W. Winnicott was a British psychiatrist and pediatrician who studied and wrote about child development. He developed a way of drawing back and forth with a child in order to initiate communication. In his 1968 essay "The Squiggle Game" he writes: "The principle is that psychotherapy is done in an overlap of the area of play of the child and the area of play of the therapist or adult. The squiggle game is one example of the way such play may be facilitated."[3] Winnicott's "Squiggle Game" is the inspiration for this game.

Most children like to draw, or at least scribble. Most parents can manage a doodle, if not a masterpiece. This activity allows parents and children to connect through the process of doodling or scribbling together. All that is required is a willingness to follow one another's lead in the drawing, and to stay focused on the process of what you are doing together instead of the drawing being produced—no need to worry if it doesn't **look** like a tree, flower, or whatever. It is about what happens between the two of you as you are drawing, and anything you do create is worthy of display on the fridge as a reminder of pleasurable time spent together.

How to play

Find a quiet area with plenty of space to sit, on the floor or at a table across from one another. Have large paper (pads of blank newsprint work well) and a variety of colored markers ready. The parent will go first by making a line, any kind of line, straight or squiggly, on the sheet of paper. The child then starts a scribble from the point where the parent's scribble ends. From here, continue back and forth, each making a scribble

---

3   Winnicott, D.W. (1968) "The Squiggle Game." In *Voices: The Art and Science of Psychotherapy 4*, 1.

starting from where the other left off. This is best done non-verbally so the two of you can really be in this creative space together without the demands of conversation. Try making the marks fast and then slowly, complex or simple, bold or light. Pay attention to what you notice while playing, about yourself and about the other player, and about what is happening between the two of you. When the activity feels complete, admire your scribble picture together without judgment, if you like. Set it aside and do another.

Comments on the game

Children who are newly home or whose first language is not the same as that of their adoptive parents will likely find this game engaging, as will children who are challenged by verbal communication for other reasons. By spending time in the process of drawing together, children experience parents being attentive and attuned, even though they may not be **speaking** the same language.

Children who have a high need for control may find this game frustrating at first, as they cannot predict or specify what their parent will do when it is their turn to draw. "Daddy, you were supposed to put ears on the elephant, not a mustache!" Over time, playing the game can help build trust in the connection the two of you share, and build tolerance for the differences between the two of you as well.

CHILD AS PARENT

Contributed by Deborah Gray

Age: 5 and up
Play time: 10–30 minutes

When we get in touch with the thoughts and feelings of others, we are able to connect better. This is a fun activity as the child practices being the parent, while the parent acts at being the child. Most parents like the chance to view things from the point of view of a child. Children love giving structure and helping their "children" with food, calming, etc. Often we gain new insights into children when we play this game.

How to play

Parent and child set the timer, deciding how long to play the game. The child can decide whether to dress up for the occasion or not. It is their choice. We usually want to leave some dress-up details to the imagination, which helps with children's mental development. Then we decide what activities to do. Usually it is a mealtime or playtime. The parent's job is to act like the child, without being so overly dramatic that kids are overwhelmed. For example, the parent might say that she wants to play jump rope, but she does not want to eat right now; she will come back later. Then the child has to decide whether or not that is a good idea. The parent can use sotto voice, "I wonder if she will make me finish eating everything before I play? Should I yell—or not? Do you think that she will make me have a time out if I yell? Should I try to calm down and agree to eating first, playing in just a minute?"

Children love being the ones to structure time and give reasons for behavior. Sometimes they get frustrated with their "child's" behavior.

It is fascinating to see how much of our parental behavior they copy. This game helps with attachment. The parent (playing the child) can remind herself that her mother does love her. She looks at the child, who is acting as parent, and says that the parent has her best interests at heart. For example, "I know that my mom loves me and just wants me to eat my lunch so I won't be hungry later. OK, I will do it."

In play both parent and child are able to express things that produce attachment.

Comments on the game

This game allows parents and children to increase their insight into each other's motivations and behaviors. It helps with the development of a "theory of mind" as mentioned in Chapter 1. It can be a fun method of trying on each other's roles—and it is a great way to help children to practice and understand some of the positive ways parents nurture and structure.

WRITING BACK AND FORTH

Contributed by Deborah Gray

Age: 9 and up—including teens

Activity time: 30 minutes

Sometimes our relationships become strained with the day-to-day struggles over homework and routines. When we try to smooth things, everything seems to be taken the wrong way. This activity helps to re-establish connection.

How to engage

There is a list of phrases at the end of this section. Each phrase should be copied onto an individual piece of paper. The papers will be folded in half and put into a basket or bowl. The parent and child or teen will each select three pieces of paper from the basket. They will omit one choice, choosing two out of the three phrases to write on. They will not share their phrases out loud. They will have two to eight minutes (depending on processing and writing speed) to write from three words to five sentences on a separate piece of paper for each phrase selected.

Then the parent and child/teen will take turns sharing what is on their piece of paper. If they do not want to share, they can still listen to what the other has to share. Often teens who are not sure that they want to share aloud, will decide to do so once they hear that their parent's sharing is not critical and shaming. Sometimes the exchange is not done verbally. The parent and teen will simply exchange their writings.

Phrases

- The things I value about my son/daughter are…

- When I felt like people cared more for me than just my performance was…

- What I worry about for my future is…

- What I have a hard time doing is…

- My hope for us in five years is…

- When I lose my temper with you, I feel…

- When I can't express how I feel, I feel…

- When people don't listen to me, I feel…

- What gives me confidence in our future together is…

- I feel the most love for you when…

- A son/daughter is…

- A mother is…

- A father is…

- I am sad when I think of…

- I can feel my love for you most when…

- When I think of getting older I feel…

People can also make up topics of their own, or they can simplify the phrases into feeling words like: love…anger…shame…pride… helping…loneliness.

Comments on the activity

This activity is one for re-opening communication and connection. The phrases in the basket allow people to move beyond the trivia of daily demands. They are able to talk about the positives and strains of their relationship. I have found this especially powerful with teens who are struggling with connection and independence at the same time. It gives parents a chance to affirm their love for their teens. Often teens will respond in a caring manner.

Chapter 4

Connecting the Whole Family

BURRITO

Contributed by Julie Fisher

Age: All ages
Play time: 5–10 minutes

The best part of this game is that it works for everyone, young and old. It takes "swaddling" to new, playful heights. All you need to play this game is a blanket and your imagination. Usually parents introduce this game, but once children know it, they are likely to request it frequently. "Burrito" has the advantage of not only being fun to play, but also calming children through pressure. It has the additional advantage of helping lead children to an awareness of foods, potentially leading to desensitization. For children with food troubles, just *imagining* that one might actually eat beans can get them a few steps closer to touching, and eventually tasting, a bean.

How to play

A parent or older child can grab a blanket nearby—keeping a large, sturdy blanket in your living room is a good idea for many games—and spread it out on the floor. The parent can help the children decide who should go first as the primary burrito ingredient. That child or parent lies down on the blanket about 18 inches/45cm from the edge, with her head mostly off the blanket. The rest of the family playing the game surrounds the person on the blanket to "make" the burrito. Going around the circle, each family member takes a turn to say what he is putting on the burrito (cheese, sour cream, lettuce, beans, etc.). While applying the topping, the burrito maker can lightly or firmly—depending on how the "burrito" likes to be touched—touch the person lying down, while shaking, tossing, or squeezing out the ingredient. Once all decide that the burrito is "ready," the parent and older children help roll it up, gently turning the person inside over a few times until he or she is bundled up. Be sure the burrito can breathe! Once the burrito is made, the rest of the family can pretend to eat the burrito and exclaim how wonderful it tastes. This is a great time for the parent to be extra playful, saying things like, "That one is spicy!" or pretend burping loudly and saying "Excuse me!" in a theatrical voice. Once that burrito is "eaten," it is time to see who wants to be the next one!

Comments on the game

Although this game is called "Burrito," families have been known to take it in all different culinary directions. Your family may decide to go with all sweets or all breakfast-time toppings. In this instance, you could call it "Crepes." Part of the fun is allowing for each participant's creativity in the making of the burrito—and in the end, it's something that you all made together.

Children get a particular kick out of seeing that their parent can get into a physical game like "Burrito," and being the burrito yourself gives you a chance to model even more playfulness. You can say, "Oh no, not hot sauce! Don't make it too hot!" Or "Okay, it's your burrito, I guess olives are okay. Maybe if I keep trying them, I'll like olives someday." For children who are too big for swaddling, this blanket game is the perfect opportunity to experience the comfort and soothing that comes with being bundled up. This is also a game that gets everyone moving.

Engaging in large motor movement is good for connection, exercise, and changing moods. Sometimes the very best way to reset a child's "bad mood" is to grab a blanket, get down on the floor, and shift gears while being smothered in sour cream!

HOT DOG HUGS

Contributed by Deborah Gray

Age: All ages
Play time: 1–5 minutes

Children of all ages like "hot dog hugs." The parents are the "bun," their children may choose being the "hot dog, mustard, pickle" or other condiment. This game includes everyone in the family in a quick expression of closeness. This fun, attachment-forming activity raises self-esteem and connection for all family members as they feel pleasure at being part of their family. After all, all of us love to be included in a fun, welcoming group! This is a spontaneous game. You can call out "hot dog hug" if you notice your family could seize the moment to celebrate. Or you can use the time to improve the day, perhaps balancing a nerve-jarring commute or transition.

How to play

Someone in the family, usually the parent, calls out, "hot dog hug!" Family members join in, announcing their favorite positions. For example: "I am one side of the bun. I am the hot dog. I am the onions. I am the mustard. I am the ketchup." Single parents extend their arms and legs to be both sides of the bun.

Parents then lightly squeeze their "hot dogs." Or they might say, "Is the ketchup spread around?" They squeeze a little more, or wiggle to get the "ketchup" spread. Children who like and need deep pressure in the form of tight hugs will giggle and say, "More." Parents can gauge the amount of pressure by the return pressure of their children. If kids squirm uncomfortably, or throw their elbows out, back off. If they wiggle pleasurably and hug back, the pressure is fine.

While hugging, parents can add, "Who has the best hot dog, or ketchup, in the world?" Of course the answers, as supplied by you or your children, are "I do!" or "You do!" or "We do!" Some playful parents can pretend that they want to take a "nibble" or "little taste," moving into a little game of catch or a little tickle game. (Only use the "nibble" suggestion if your children know you well enough not to be afraid.)

Comments on the game

This is a super game to play just before dinner. It helps to keep everyone connected and relaxed as they sit down to eat. (If you have wiggly children who stand or sit on one leg to eat, the discharge of excess energy might allow them to actually sit at dinner.) Eating together is attachment-forming, so playing "hot dog hug" primes the family for more enjoyment as they move into another attachment-producing experience.

Children in the family who have sensitivities to pressure are able to control the amount of pressure, teaching their parents and others the amount of sensory pressure that feels enjoyable. If your children are getting irritable, this game will help them to feel better balanced (regulated) by connection with you—and with the pleasant pressure from the hugs.

BALL PLAY

Contributed by Julie Fisher

Age: Infant to 5 years
Play time: 1–5 minutes

Aside from parents, the ball is the best toy around. Balls can be thrown, tossed, rolled, bounced, juggled, dribbled, dunked, smashed, and hidden. Balls come in all shapes, weights and sizes. Having a ball handy is a good strategy for connecting with children. In particular, having a small inflatable beach ball is a great way to have a ball always close by. A beach ball has the added bonus of not hurting others when thrown. Also, similar to a balloon, the excitement and anticipation in watching a ball come to life adds to the shared enjoyment of ball play.

How to play

Once you have a ball and enough people for a game, it's nice to start out in a circle on the floor. For younger children, especially, it's useful to make a closed circle with everyone's legs forming the "walls" and with feet touching. This provides a natural boundary for keeping the ball within your shared space. The parent can begin by rolling the ball to one of the children in the circle. One way to connect everyone playing the game is to sing about what you are doing. The parent can say, "I roll the ball to Susie, and she rolls it back to me" in a sing-song voice. If Susie rolls the ball elsewhere, the parent can say, "I roll the ball to Susie, and she rolls it over to Johnny." The singing helps with engagement and inclusion, and it usually doesn't take long for others to catch on to the play and the singing.

Often children will want to vary the action of the ball from rolling to throwing. This is a splendid opportunity to practice the appropriate force for ball throwing in the house—and it is in the variations that happen, from rolling, to throwing, to bouncing, etc., that the game gets extra playful. In the moment of back-and-forth with the ball, new ideas spring to life and jump from player to player.

One participant, probably an adult, may suggest using a basket for throwing the ball into, for example. This gives the opportunity for lots of celebrating when anyone "makes it." Additionally, the ball can be used to keep a conversation going or to invite creativity. Whoever has the ball might have to call out a color. This adds to the intrigue for older siblings who are playing. For babies and young toddlers, the vocal exchanges while rolling the ball with a parent are likely to be squeals of delight and other non-verbal sounds that indicate joy and connection. Small babies can be propped in the "V" of an older sibling or parent's legs in order to participate more fully.

Comments on the game

A ball is a conversation starter. It provides the focus for interaction and the simplicity of a shared goal: to keep it going, to know where it is. From keeping your eye on the ball to making eye contact, there is a natural continuation. Because rolling a ball is a concrete representation of back-and-forth connection, it can be a good way to practice learning a baby or toddler's cues for engagement and disengagement; when a baby is tired of the game, the ball is not headed back your way, or may not even be anywhere in sight. Like other simple games, particularly when using an inflatable ball, it is easy to be ready for beginning and ending ball play in a variety of settings and spaces. Perhaps it is no accident that one of the early words for many toddlers is "ball." A toy this great should be easy to say, easy to request.

Figure 4.1: Ball play

"RING AROUND THE ROSY"

Contributed by Julie Fisher

Age: Toddler to 8 years
Play time: 1–10 minutes

"Ring around the rosy" is another of those classic nursery rhymes that children love. It is a rich game for connection because it contains three wonderful elements: singing, hand-holding, and movement. It can be used to "switch gears" for young children, as a ritual for coming and going, and as a way to build bonds through shared experience.

There is a myth that "Ring around the rosy" originates from the time of the Black Plague. According to Snopes.com, this is unlikely. The first noted recording of this nursery rhyme was in the late 1800s, hundreds of years after the Black Plague of the 1300s or the lesser plague of the 1600s, so most historians do not actually believe it is referencing plagues and death.

How to play

To play, form a circle and join hands. Everyone moves in the same direction in a circle, singing "Ring around the rosy, pocket full of posies, ashes, ashes, we all fall down!" Once down on the ground, a second verse can be sung to bring everyone back to their feet: on their knees, everyone slowly taps the ground, alternating hands and singing, "The cows are in the meadow, eating buttercups, THUNDER [slap hands faster against the ground], LIGHTNING [again, fast hand-slapping], we all stand up!" As everyone gets up, usually the participants will want to do it again, so just repeat the singing, going around in a circle, falling down, and getting back up again, until everyone is too tired or uninterested to continue.

Comments on the game

"Ring around the rosy" is a game that can be used to signify the beginning and end of playtime together. Having rituals can assist children for whom transitions are extra challenging. Children enjoy this game from as soon as they can walk until around age eight, sometimes even later than that. Many children are excited by the "thunder" and "lightning" part of standing back up. This is another nice game for bonding older and younger siblings, and for older siblings to feel that they are "in the know" as to how to engage in the game correctly, and thus able to teach the younger crowd. "Ring around the rosy" also provides an opportunity for physical closeness and plenty of giggles. As parents and children fall to the ground together and get back up together, there are opportunities for hugs and squeezes and abundant silliness. Participants can be dramatic in their falling and getting back up; the group can practice singing loudly and then singing softly. Sometimes older siblings will want to go too fast in moving the circle around. This can create an opportunity to build empathy for how that feels to shorter legs that cannot keep up the pace.

As an added benefit, this game helps to wake up tired parents. It can be difficult to keep your energy level high and your spirit engaged. Working into your play routine games like "Ring around the rosy" allows for regular opportunities to get your blood pumping. We also know movement is helpful for building attachment in children; so everyone wins with this classic nursery rhyme game of falling down and rising up together.

HIDE-AND-SEEK

Contributed by Julie Fisher

Age: All ages
Play time: 5–30 minutes

Around age four, many children become enthralled with the classic game of hide-and-seek. What makes this game particularly wonderful for connecting the family is its adaptability for all ages and skill levels. For younger children, hide-and-seek may not involve leaving a space where everyone is; or it may mean being part of a team with an older sibling or parent. Additionally, hide-and-seek does not have to involve a person hiding. A version that can be played even in a doctor's waiting room, involves hiding a small object, as opposed to people hiding/relocating (the more usual version of the game).

How to play

The traditional way to play hide-and-seek is to have someone who is "it" who covers her eyes and counts to an agreed number, say 20. Once that number is reached, that person calls out, "Ready or not, here I come!" and then goes to search for the people who are hiding. It is a good idea to decide ahead of time the parameters for where hiding can take place (only the house, only the main floor, only the yard, etc.). It can also be good to specify what happens when someone is found—are they "it" now? Do they help the seeker find the others? Can the others run to a "base" if they can get there without being caught? There are many ways to set up the rules. To connect everyone, the growing seeker group can find each person who is still hiding and then determine, once everyone is found, who should be "it" next. One of the benefits of hide-and-seek is that it can be played indoors or outdoors and no equipment is needed. This game can be played in teams, which is a nice way to bond family members around a common goal, as well as involve the youngest children in the family.

A variation of this game involves hiding a small object either on a person or in an area of a room. In this variation, the person who is "it" leaves the room while the item is being hidden—or if that is not possible, as is the case in a small, crowded doctor's waiting room, there is always the classic game "Which hand is it in?" that involves the hider choosing a hand to hide the item in (behind his back), and then the guesser saying in which hand he thinks it is located.

Another such game in the hide-and-seek family of games is "I spy." In "I spy," the "spyer" sees something and says "I spy with my little eye something that is green" (or whatever color), and then the guesser has to look around and ask questions or make guesses. "I spy" is another quick, easy game that can be used to connect with children in small spaces and at times when proactively connecting can make a big difference for everyone's experience of a stressful time (such as waiting in line at the grocery store).

Comments on the game

Hide-and-seek is about being sought and found. By its very nature, it lends itself to powerful connection. It is a reunion game. So much of attachment is experienced in the coming and going in life. Many children with traumatic early relationship experiences do not have a positive template for hello and good-bye. There is also a rich opportunity with hide-and-seek to explore boundaries and test rules. If a child is new to your home and you are not sure roaming will feel safe (for you or her), that is a good time to think about playing in teams, or to be ready for orchestrating the game so as not to be too far away; it can feel safer to limit the space more drastically for children who cannot or should not be too far away from you. The classic hide-and-seek moment for a younger child is when she hides in a **very** obvious, non-hidden space—and that is another part of the beauty of hide-and-seek: imagination and suspending disbelief come into play.

An additional benefit to hide-and-seek is the working together part. When playing on teams, you are counting, seeking, sharing anticipation, and building memories. An important part of feeling like part of a family (or any social group) is having shared experiences. Due to the exciting nature of hide-and-seek, it naturally "sticks" in your child's brain as one of those meaningful connection memories.

Yet another gift of this game is the spatial and tactile awareness and learning that can come with it. Do I fit in this space? How about this box in this closet? What does it feel like when I am this close to the shower curtain? And of course, there is the regulatory benefit that comes with moving your body and employing your large muscle groups.

Finally, the less involved "cousins" of hide-and-seek (hiding an object; "I spy") still give the players the benefit of connection through creativity, curiosity, and anticipation. Having a shared goal—where *is* that item? What green thing can she possibly mean?—piques the curiosity and wakes up the mind for sharing and connection; and that is the key to why hide-and-seek is so excellent for attachment.

Figure 4.2: Hide-and-seek

WHO IS IN THIS FAMILY?

Contributed by Julie Fisher

Age: 3 and up

Play time: 3–5 minutes

Children with attachment disruptions often display indiscriminate affection; they will want to go to anyone, to sit in stranger's laps. This is a safety-seeking behavior that should be addressed. We want children to know who their parents and siblings are, and to prefer family above all others. "Who is in this family?" is a game for addressing this need.

How to play

This game works best when there is someone visiting who is not in the family, though it can be adapted for play by using dolls, puppets, or stuffed animals to represent strangers or acquaintances. To play, the parent starts a conversation about who is in the family. Children call out names and the parent focuses on names of those who are present for the game. If someone from outside the family is present, then that person becomes the "other." If stand-ins are being used (dolls, etc.), those stand-ins are given names of acquaintances or deemed "strangers."

Next, the family members stand up, lock arms, and form a huddle. If there is a human "other" present, that person gently tries to "break into" the family huddle. The family members say things like, "Nope, sorry, you are not part of this family! For family members only!" The person trying to break in can plead with the family members. She can say things like, "But I'm very nice! I see you every other week when I visit your house!" The family holds steady and this sequence is repeated a few times until the "intruder" retreats, saying something like "I get it now. I know this family a little, but I am not *in* this family. I have my own family. I don't live here. I'm just a visitor who will go home soon."

If there is no outside person present, the parent and older siblings can say things like, "Mr. Johnson [the stuffed bunny] is over there on the couch because he's not part of this family," and "Billy over there thinks he should be in the circle because he mows our lawn, but he's not in our family, either!" Parents can repeat the names of who is in the family and ask questions with pretty obvious answers, such as, "Is your teacher in our family?" and "What about Superman, is he in our family?" These silly questions can stretch the play and get children contributing things like, "No, but Superman could swoop in from above!" Then the family can make sure they get closer so that there is no room for Superman to enter the circle from above, etc.

Comments on the game

"Who is in this family?" provides an opportunity to physically represent an important story that bears repeating over and over. It emphasizes "you are a part of us, you belong, you are wanted!" When there is another person as the "other," having that person witness this proclamation adds to the power of the message. Children love repetition and love hearing they are loved and wanted. This game connects the family literally and plays on the idea of a team, as in football huddles. An additional way to drive this point home is to have large photos of all family members on the wall in one of the main rooms in the home. Above the photos can be a sign saying: "Our Family." While playing the game, the parent can reference the photographic "evidence" on the wall for the proclamations made regarding family membership.

FAMILY CIRCLE

Contributed by Laura Stone

Age: 3 and up
Play time: 5–10 minutes

All of us, at one time or another, need to be embraced and reminded that we belong. Some children will join their families directly from institutional care, with little or no experience of family life. Other children who have had a chaotic start in their first families will also need to learn what it means to have a place in a safe and stable family. Creating an actual circle on the ground with all the family members inside of it can help kids to really get what it means to be *in* the family.

How to play

Take a long length of nylon (not rough) rope or cord and form a circle on the ground. Get the whole family seated or standing inside the circle. Talk about this safe circle that is your family, who belongs in it, what it means to you, why it is important. Make this a positive discussion; the point is not to exclude others but to help children realize that the people in the circle belong together in a special way, and will remain connected to one another. Experiment with making the circle bigger and smaller, and stay inside. Notice with kids how the circle can expand and contract, but you are all still inside. If the rope should separate, show how it can be brought together again. If children run out of the circle, call them back. If they are uncomfortable being in the circle, notice that and talk a little bit about it. Let them play close to the circle for a while. Invite them in again. Wait a while and play the game another day; play often until they can be inside the circle with you.

Another way to work with this activity is to draw it out. Draw a circle and write the names of immediate family members inside. Draw an outer circle around the first one. In this circle, write the names of people close to your family—grandparents, good friends, close neighbors, and so forth. If you like, draw another circle around the second one and include here the names of others you know but who are more distant friends.

Comments on the game

This is an excellent activity for children who are new in the home. It is also helpful for those children who tend to try to engage strangers but don't always seem to stay connected with their own families. Try playing before an outing to help kids remember who their "people" are in highly stimulating public settings.

FAMILY PHOTO PUZZLE

Contributed by Laura Stone

Age: 5 and up

Play time: 30 minutes

Jigsaw puzzles are great fun and can help little hands and eyes work together to connect seemingly random parts. What satisfaction there is in finally completing the picture! In this activity family photographs are applied to the puzzle pieces and children and parents get to work together to form the picture.

How to play

On a large piece of card stock or tag board, use mod podge, acrylic medium or other craft glue to create a photo montage (a collection of pictures) of your family. The more pictures the better. Coat the final image a few times with the medium, allowing it to dry between coats, in order to get the pieces firmly in place. Once it is dry, draw jigsaw shapes lightly in pencil over the image—make the shapes large or small, many or few, as suits your family's ability and patience with puzzles. Use an Exacto knife (craft knife) or scissors (parents only) to cut the image into jigsaw pieces, using the pencil marks as a guide. Mix up the pieces. Spend time piecing your puzzle together: shake it up in a box or zippered bag, dump it out and put it together again. Try making another puzzle using a family drawing for the image.

Optional: If you are handy with technology, create the montage in a software program and print it out. There are also many online options for ordering a puzzle using your photos, but it is more fun to do your own at home.

Comments on the game

Puzzles can be very comforting for young children, as they require them to *puzzle* over the right order, understand relationship, and ultimately achieve mastery by fitting the pieces together. For children who haven't had many toys or chances to try things for themselves, putting puzzles together can be soothing and pleasurable.

This activity again visually reinforces the idea of family as a group of people who are special to one another and belong together. It also shows how family can be cohesively formed from parts that may individually appear very different.

STORY ROUNDS

Contributed by Laura Stone

Age: 5 and up
Play time: 30 minutes

Camp fires, long car rides, even waiting at the doctor's office can all be opportunities to connect and reinforce family ties through story games. Parents can create a kind of cocoon around the family in all sorts of settings by engaging children in storytelling, inviting them to use their imagination and focus their attention on what is happening in the family dialogue. The stories created also make great memories for parents and children.

How to play

Have the family members sit in a circle. The parent starts a story, saying about three to five beginning lines, such as "Once upon a time, on a dark and stormy night, a tiny mouse sat in a tiny overstuffed chair and looked out his tiny window from his tiny mousehole in the wall of the old red barn…" The next family member says the next few lines and details of the story, making them up on the spot, such as "Imagine how surprised the mouse was to see the foot of an enormous dinosaur lumbering along just beyond the garden gate…" Parents can tone things down during their turn if kids begin to include bits that are too scary. Continue in a round, for as many rounds as desired, with the parent finishing the story on a soothing note. Make it funny, high drama, fantastical, gentle, as suits the needs of the family at that moment. If you create a favorite story, tell it again sometimes. Tell it until you all remember it by heart.

Comments on the game

This game allows children to feel intimately connected to a part of their parent's mind, and to be witnessed in their own creative thoughts and internal experiences by their parents. When children are free and encouraged to express their ideas, and parents are able to hear and connect with children through those ideas, there is safe and perhaps sacred space created in the minds of both child and parent. Children come to feel known and accepted by parents, and develop trust that the parents will "hold" them and keep them in their minds, and will help them to manage overwhelming thoughts and feelings. Stories can become a powerful tool for children for self-soothing during periods of brief separation, as the child can recall both the story and the shared space in which the story was created.

FAMILY COOKBOOK

Contributed by Laura Stone

Age: 5 and up
Play time: varies

Food is such a central part of family life, and we tend to think of coming together as a family around the main meal of the day. However, many children will enter their families with a background that includes hunger or malnutrition. Some children from other countries may find the food in their new home tastes funny at first, and they may miss the food they had in their previous home. Through preparing food and eating together, with the needs of each member in mind, families can create a point of connection and establish an atmosphere of nurturing, understanding, and security. This activity provides an opportunity for each family member to get creative and to have their favorites noted and included, which lets them know they belong and that their wants and needs are important.

How to play

Collect a number of recipes (maybe eight to ten) that are favorites of the family. Include at least one favorite for each family member, even if the others don't care for the dish. Be sure to include lots of dishes that kids this age can make on their own (peanut butter toast, rice cereal treats, etc.) Make sure to have some variety in the recipes: breakfasts, lunches, dinners, treats. Parents will type up the recipes, and kids can draw pictures or take photos to include. Put together a cookbook using a book cover report or a ring-binder. Be sure to title it with your family name(s). Display proudly and use often. Send a copy to close friends and relatives—what a fun gift.

Comments on the game

As children grow older and more capable of cooking on their own, they may add recipes that they have tested and that have been approved by the family. Cooking is an important life skill and preparing meals for the family is a terrific way to practice independence while still staying connected. Preparing food can be a way to explore and celebrate the cultures within your multicultural family. Your cookbook may grow to include favorite holiday or special occasion recipes as well. For children who need help with making healthy choices, the recipes chosen can reflect nutritional needs and include suggestions on reasonable portion sizes.

QUILT OF QUESTIONS

Contributed by Laura Stone

Age: 5 and up

Play time: an hour to make, 20–30 minutes to play

Families take form in lots of different ways. The members of a family may or may not resemble one another, but they are connected to each other to form a unit. Quilts are sewn together from lots of small pieces of possibly all kinds of stuff—bits of clothes, old or new fabrics, even other quilts. Quilts are objects of comfort and warmth, and they often tell a story through their patterns and designs. Here is an activity to do with your family to celebrate all the different "stuff" you are made of, to express your creativity in an easy and fun way, and to tell your family story.

How to play

You will need a large piece of poster board or foam core, about 18"x 24" (45cm x 60cm). Use a pencil to draw a grid on the board, creating even-sized shapes (think of a patchwork quilt). You can use all squares or triangles, or get more complex—but don't make the pieces smaller than about 3"x 3" (8cm x 8cm). Make an "x" lightly to mark the front side of each shape. Cut the shapes out using scissors or an Exacto (craft) knife (parents only). Color the back of each shape any way you like using paint, colored pencils or markers, or glue on colored paper (see Figure 4.3). On the front side, write a question related to the family, e.g. "How old was — when he lost his first tooth?" or "What is Mom's favorite flower?" or "When did — join the family?" Put the quilt together as a family, color-side up, in any order or configuration that pleases you. Take turns flipping a piece over and answering the question. Get help from other family members if you need it. Turn the piece back over and have the next person take a turn. Play until all or most of the pieces have been turned over. Store the pieces and play again another day.

Comments on the game

By "weaving" together the quilt squares, and playing with the configurations, families are exploring and affirming the flexibility of their boundaries and connection. Each of the pieces is unique and yet they fit together in the game, as do the members of the family. There is no one right way—things can change and yet still be cohesive. Everyone has different likes and dislikes, everyone has their own story both apart from and within the story of the family.

Figure 4.3: Quilt of questions

FAMILY PIE

Contributed by Laura Stone

Age: 5 and up

Play time: an hour or more (varies)

For kids who like arts and crafts, this activity provides lots of satisfaction. It involves the construction of an elaborate, pie-shaped, family-made, one-of-a-kind work of art that can be displayed at home. While the finished product requires the whole family working together, each individual family member's contribution can be seen in the piece.

This is an activity that will require some patience, as there are some complex parts that take a while to complete. Parents can certainly help children complete their portions of the drawing, but it is important that everybody gets to put their own mark(s) on the drawing. The idea here is to create something all together as a family that will highlight and bring together each person's contribution. The concentric circle shapes help reinforce the idea of the "family circle" as well.

How to play

This activity will require use of a circle compass, or you can use round objects like plates to make concentric circles. Find the center on a large (18" x 24" (45cm x 60cm) or larger) piece of thick paper or posterboard. Mark the center and create a series of concentric circles around it, making the space between circles at least 1.5" (3cm) (See Figure 4.4). Make as many circles as you have family members. Now draw a line through the center point vertically, and another horizontally, to create four quadrants, as if you were going to cut a pie into four equal pieces. If you have lots of family members, divide the pie into as many pieces as there are family members. If you have a really big family, start with a really big pie.

Now have each family member draw a pattern in one of the concentric circles, to fill that circle all the way around. Try to create a pattern using outlines of shapes without filling them in. For example, one person might choose the second circle from the center and create a leaf pattern all the way around by drawing outlines of leaf shapes. If leaf shapes prove too difficult or frustrating, try polka dots or heart shapes. Little ones can just do dots, or even rubber stamps that they choose.

When each family member has drawn in their circle, each person chooses one slice of the pie to color, so that each family member colors in a "slice," which will include a section of all the patterns drawn by all the family members. You may need to take turns so as not to bump each other's hands too much while drawing and coloring.

When it is done you will have a unique, tapestry-like drawing that you have all created together. Hang up your pie. Admire it. See how the shapes and colors are interwoven.

Comments on the game

Kids love to look at this project and see their parts as parts of the whole. If it turns out well, kids may come and look at the image when they are having a hard time, as a way to focus and calm down. Rainy and snowy days are a good time to work on this project. It is also a fun activity to do outside with sidewalk chalk on a sunny day. Be sure to take a photograph before it rains!

Figure 4.4: Family pie

FAMILY SHIELD

Contributed by Deborah Gray

Age: All ages
Play time: 1–2 hours

Most of us want family members to feel proud to be a part of the family. When we think of our family strengths it makes us feel good about belonging to a great team. We feel more capable of facing everyday life. This activity creates a royal shield, with symbols to help families identify their core qualities. When finished, the shield can be hung on the wall.

How to play

You will need a large piece of tag board. Cut it into the shape of a shield. Depending on the age and talents of family members, this can range from a simple, round shape to a complex shape. Talk as a family about the things that make the family special. Look at some classic family shields with their emblems, in a book or online, generating some ideas for your family. For example, your family values and emblems might be courage, faith, and caring. Or you might have strength, sharing, and education. Talk about some symbols that illustrate those concepts. Discuss ways to work family members' names into the designs. Some families like to cut out or draw animals or landscapes to work into the pattern. The words and drawings can be done on separate paper, either colored or white. You can use pictures from magazines as well.

It is an important part of the process to have everyone's ideas represented. If you have family members who are less flexible, you can divide the shield into parts, with different members in charge of the various sections.

Then, family members place the words and pictures on the shield. Everything is arranged and then glued down. The family shield hangs as a reminder for the whole family—a symbol of its best characteristics.

Comments on the game

This activity helps build self-esteem in the whole family. Sometimes we spend too much time thinking about what is wrong with our families, or just about the logistics of getting through the day's events. This activity helps everyone think about the values and positives of the family. It gives expression for people with artistic talents, and those who are good at word-finding. It gives options for lots of shared decision-making, as well as a process that lets people work individually on a section before putting it into the final product.

Chapter 5

Connecting Siblings

FORTS

Contributed by Laura Stone

> Age: 3 and up
> Play time: from 10 minutes to all day

Most of us probably remember building forts or other cozy spaces out of pillows and blankets as young children, and feeling as if we were in our own little world inside of them. Siblings who are new to each other may enjoy creating such special spaces together and claiming them as their shared pretend world. Parents can help by providing safe materials and guiding kids just enough to work out the structural details. Store-bought play tents are fine, but half the fun is building the structure and fixing it when it falls apart. Parents will want to be able to see and hear what is going on in the fort, while also allowing enough privacy for kids to enjoy imaginative play.

How to play

Gather some large pillows, an old sheet or thin blanket, some safe support structures such as small chairs or tables, and perhaps some clothes pins or clips. If necessary, demonstrate how to build a play space with these materials. Be sure kids are creating an exit door and that nobody is getting trampled inside. Most children will quickly get the idea. Kids who haven't had much opportunity to do such activities before may need additional help to get started. Minor squabbles are to be expected, and parents can view these as part of the process of siblings connecting to one another. Parents can read a story to kids inside the tent or kids may want to read to each other or listen to music. If allowed, kids can share a snack inside as well. Parents should remain nearby, but reserve the fort for sibling play only.

Comments on the game

Creating a shared space in the middle of the livingroom floor allows new siblings to create meaningful shared space in their minds as they play. When parents facilitate such play opportunities for siblings they are sending the message that these connections are unique and important, and children feel safe and free to explore these new relationships.

BODY TRACINGS

Contributed by Laura Stone

Age: 5 and up

Play time: 20 minutes

Have you ever heard a young child, perhaps your own, remark to a new person, "You have a funny nose!" or some such awkward observation? Finding differences and similarities between ourselves and others is part of discovering and relating. Children who are new to one another will most certainly notice all sorts of things about each other and will need to process these observations in the initial stages of making meaningful and deep connections. This activity provides a way for new siblings to process in a visual and "concrete" manner what they see and notice about each other.

How to play

You will need some very large paper, such as bulletin board paper, that can be rolled out on the floor. Markers or felt tip pens work best for tracing. Roll out enough paper so that each child can lie down on the paper. In pairs have one child trace the outline of the other and continue until all children are traced. Have the kids color in the tracings of each other, noticing and writing what they see in the margins. Encourage them to be kind and not critical, but also candid, e.g. "My sister has brown eyes, not blue like mine," or "Zach wears hearing aids to help him hear," and "We both have brown hair." Help children find differences and similarities on the outside and on the inside. "I think my brother has a big brain because he knows algebra," or "My sister has a big heart even though she gets mad sometimes, like me." "We both like soccer." Images can be put up on the walls for a while and added to as new discoveries are made.

Comments on the game

Some children are not used to being seen in this way and for them, at first, the exercise may feel like too much. Try going slow, perhaps leaving off the words and sticking with just coloring in the tracings at first. Instead of hanging up the pictures, set them aside in a safe place and take them out to look at them sometimes. Come back to the pictures another day and have a sibling add a compliment or a note of accomplishment: "Today Nina got her first happy face sticker at school."

Try doing the drawings again over time. Compare last year's drawings to this year's; notice how children have grown to know and understand each other more deeply.

THE STORY OF...

Contributed by Julie Fisher

Age: 5 and up
Play time: 10–60 minutes

Children who have experienced trauma often have a harder time differentiating themselves from others. They also struggle with self-esteem. This activity is meant to help with these things. It is an intentional way for siblings to define themselves and understand each other better. As a parent, providing the time, materials, and space for this activity is just another way to give the clear message, "You matter."

How to play

For this activity you will need poster boards or bulletin boards, one for each child. You will also need glue, tape, or pushpins to attach things to the boards. The child, with help from the parent and siblings, will use the board to tell about him or herself. It is a storytelling board. What does he like? What is her favorite color? What things are unique about him? Pictures from magazines, actual photographs, words written on paper (for example, "SILLY")—anything goes. The point is for individualization and celebration of difference. Once the boards are started, they are hung somewhere in the house, together, or if the child prefers or because space is limited, each board is hung in each child's bedroom or personal space. Over time, things get added to the board. The emphasis, however, is on uniqueness and difference. These storyboards are a way to call out how everyone is different and how the family celebrates and accepts each child for who he or she is.

Comments on the game

By making space for "The story of..." boards, a clear message is given. We are each unique, and that is celebrated in this home. This activity helps, particularly when there is a great deal of sibling rivalry and unrest.

Parents set the expectation for greater acceptance and it clarifies the message that **all** of the children are important. Parents can model their own healthy self-esteem by having boards, too. As these boards become a part of the family culture, siblings might find things that remind them of their brothers or sisters and then ask that sibling if she would like to put that thing on her board. For example, "I know how much you like purple, Marie, so I found this pretty purple ribbon. Do you want it for your board?" In this way, siblings can further support and reinforce the messages about individuality and specialness and keep the celebrations going over time.

Variations on this idea can be used to connect individual children to birth families and their pasts before they were in your home. When visits with birth parents are happening, children can have "visit boxes" (something as simple as a shoebox covered in wrapping paper works) in which they put things like artwork to share with parents at their next visit.

After adoption, having a special memory box for each child in your home who has birth family keepsakes and treasures (often kept in a safe place for when the child is older), is a way to help emphasize stories and represent who each child is, individually. The idea of connecting siblings involves connection to self first. Children, like adults, need to have clarity regarding who they are as individuals to help them connect with others.

QUESTS AND ADVENTURES

Contributed by Laura Stone

Age: 5 and up
Play time: from 20 minutes to all day

As humans we tend to resonate with tales of adventure. Every culture includes folktales and stories of heroes and heroines who must face obstacles and solve riddles in order to save the day. Most children play out these stories naturally whenever they can. New siblings can be helped and encouraged to create their own stories of adventure, in which they are each other's allies and must work together, drawing on each other's strengths and helping each other through weaknesses, in order to emerge victorious.

How to play

Parents can set up the play initially, with something like, "Children, I need you to retrieve the Magical Golden Elixir [the vegetable oil] from the Cavern of the Red Dragon [the back of the red car in the garage]. Beware of the traps [the empty boxes] that lie in your path. And John, take care not to let your brother fall under the spell of the Screaming Banshee [the TV] on your way! Hurry, it is almost time to make the Magical Potion [dinner]!" Feel free to make it very dramatic, but keep it at your children's comprehension level, and don't make it too scary. Props are helpful. Utilize toys and household objects such as flashlights, marbles, costumes, maps, and so forth. The quest can include a treasure hunt, with hidden objects to find along the way. Whatever the "quest" is, it should be an attainable goal. If squabbles occur during the quest, you can remind children from the sidelines that they are to utilize their own strengths to help their siblings, "John, can you use your stone of patience to help your brother make it through the maze [the laundry room]?"

Comments on the game

Being bound to a common goal, especially a goal that sounds really fun and interesting to achieve, can help bring children of very different temperaments and personalities together. Memories are made in the play space that can help keep kids connected the rest of the time.

At home, parents will need to help kids to stay on track in sibling play. If kids get too mired in their play story or can't seem to get it to wrap up, help them quickly bring the story to a peaceful conclusion that will not trouble them later, and move on to another activity. If a child becomes very upset while playing, stop the game and help the child to calm down and come back to the present. Use techniques that work for your child, such as rocking with a parent, breathing deeply, holding a favorite teddy bear, or walking around the block if that works better.

Some children with trauma in their backgrounds may display traumatic themes in their play. You may have a child turn a storyline into one that parallels his or her own traumatic experiences; for example, a mom described how her son who was playing out a search for treasure got caught up in the perception that the pirate guarding it was a "bad guy" from his past, and he began to try to hit and kick his brother (the pirate). The mother immediately helped her son to stop playing the game, to calm his body down with deep breathing, and eventually to talk about what was going on. Later, in his therapist's office, the child was able to sort out his memory from the play theme, distinguish past from present, and reconnect in a positive way with his brother. Eventually, he was able to work through his traumatic memories with the therapist. Parents need to be alert to the possibility that some children can be "triggered" in this way, and is imperative that kids with trauma history have the help they need to work through these issues in a professional setting.

Chapter 6

Activities to Help with Mood and Flexibility

ALL AGES

RED LIGHT, GREEN LIGHT

Contributed by Laura Stone

Age: All ages
Play time: 20 minutes

This is a classic fun game that requires focused attention and challenges frustration tolerance. Children will need to pay close attention and concentrate as they coordinate their physical movements with the words they hear. If they are too impulsive and jump ahead when there is a "Red Light" they will have to move back to the starting line.

How to play

This is a game that will work best with three or more players. Define a playing field—it could be a spacious room or a space outside about the size of a sports court. For more players, allow more room. Have one person be the *caller* and stand at one end of the playing field, which will be the finish line. Have the others line up at the opposite end of the field, at the starting line. The caller will start by calling out, "Green Light!" and the other players will then advance towards the finish line. When the caller is ready he or she will call out, "Red Light!" and the advancing players must freeze in place. If anyone continues to advance towards the finish line on a Red Light, they must go back to start. The game continues in this way until someone reaches the finish line and tags the caller; now that player is the caller. Everyone except the new caller goes back to the starting line and the game begins again.

Another version of this game can be played between a parent and a young child to help with connection. In this version the parent stands on one side of the room (or yard), and the child on the other. The child says "Green Light," and the parent moves closer to the child until the child says "Red Light." If the parent moves on a Red Light the child can send the parent back to start. When the parent reaches the child, the parent makes eye contact, and there can be gentle or exuberant hugs, depending on what is needed or desired; this is an opportunity to attune. Some children may get overwhelmed by this activity and need to go slowly and come together gently at the end to feel safe. Other kids will want a bear hug. Some kids like to do it with their eyes closed for even more anticipation. It is wise to always get to the end of the game; don't stop in the middle: end with an embrace.

Comments on the game

It may be helpful to talk with children after the game and notice with them what happened while playing and how they felt. Was it easy or hard to follow the directions? What did you have to do inside to make it to the finish line? How was it to be excited and listen at the same time?

STATUES

Contributed by Laura Stone

Age: All ages

Play time: 10 minutes

This activity requires both flexibility and control, as one player is sculpted by the other into various positions and expressions that may be quite different from how he or she is actually feeling at the start. Most of us recognize that a sad face and downcast eyes indicate a low mood, and we generally conclude that the body reflects the state of the mind. In this game feelings inside may change as players are sculpted into new postures, demonstrating that the mind often follows the body. For children who tend to have difficulty sync-ing up their minds and bodies, and/or difficulty reading the expressions of others, this is an activity that can help make those connections more transparent.

How to play

Decide who will be the *statue* and who will be *sculptor*. The sculptor forms the statue into various positions—perhaps easy, perhaps difficult, perhaps funny. The sculptor can experiment to create different moods in the statue, such as smiling with open arms, or frowning with hunched shoulders. Try sculpting extreme variations in succession—from beaming smile to sinister grimace, from frog-like crouch to flying-squirrel spread. Try subtle variations also—slight adjustments to the eyebrows or the corners of the mouth. The statue does his or her best to hold the pose until the sculptor changes it to something else. Giggling is likely, but try to keep quiet and focus on the body postures. However, for sculptors who have difficulty reading facial expressions and body language in others, it may be helpful to talk through what they are sculpting as they go along and say out loud how the statue might be feeling. Switch places and have the statue do the sculpting.

Comments on the game

Children can be helped to reflect on how their mood changed as they took on these different poses: How did you feel at the start? How do you feel now? Are you surprised? Which pose was most difficult? Which one would you like to do again? When you aren't sure how you are feeling, do you think you could look for clues by observing what your body is doing? In the future, if you are having trouble with your mood, do you think it would help to try changing what you are doing with your body?

DANCE PARTY

Contributed by Laura Stone

Age: All ages
Play time: 15 minutes

Young children who lacked care or suffered trauma in the past will often have difficulty transitioning smoothly from one emotional state to another. They may have difficulty "modulating"—knowing and maintaining the appropriate reaction for a given situation. Think of the kid who completely falls apart over a broken cookie, or who is truly terrified of harmless bugs; they are having difficulty knowing what merits which reaction, and tend to react too strongly (or sometimes not strongly enough) to a given situation. These children are often overly susceptible to states of "fight, flight or freeze," and may tend to express their needs as if they were experiencing an emergency, screaming when hungry, or playing at a wild pace until they collapse in utter exhaustion instead of gradually winding down. These kids will need help to become aware of their needs and express them in a way that is less distressing for themselves and their parents. "Dance Party" is a great activity for young children who need to build skills for self-awareness and for transitioning through states of being more gracefully.

How to play

You will need a stereo or other means to play music in the room. Clear the room of furniture or obstructions. Create a quiet atmosphere with low lighting and perhaps some blankets laid out on one side of the room. Invite children to lie quietly on the blankets. Start by playing some soft music—think lullabies or soothing classical pieces. Invite children to listen for a while, then, when they are ready, to stand up and move a little, listening and swaying to the music. Parents can model use of the right amount of energy by dancing too. After a time, transition the music to a slightly more upbeat tempo, perhaps a gentle children's album or soft jazz. Invite the children to keep listening and moving, matching their dancing to the pace and rhythm of the music, and dance with them. Gradually increase the tempo and possibly the volume, until the kids (and parents) are really moving around a lot, using their whole bodies. After a while, begin to reverse, slowing the tempo. Continue to wind it down until you are back to lullabies, and invite children to return to a completely relaxed and quiet state. Encourage deep and gentle breathing. If everyone is up to it, do it all again.

Comments on the game

Parents may find that it takes some trial and error to get the right combination of music and transitions to challenge but not overwhelm their child. Some children are easily overstimulated and may not be able to follow the flow of the music at first, instead amping themselves up or shutting themselves off, or increasing or decreasing their pace at not quite the right time. Keep playing over time and use the opportunity to observe and attune to what is too much and what is not quite enough in terms of stimulation, reflecting your observations back to your child with your own words and body language.

Chapter 7

Building Attachment when Children Have Had Exposure to Toxins

JILL DZIKO

In this section I have adapted some of the previously presented games, as well as added a few new games to give parents a little extra help when thinking about attachment games and how to play them with a child who has been prenatally exposed to drugs and/or alcohol.

As the parent of a child on the Fetal Alcohol Spectrum and an adoption social worker, I experience the unique challenges and joys of parenting and working with these children on a daily basis. I remember, when my daughter was about three, attending a workshop on the difference between "giraffe" and "lion" parents. "Giraffe" parents were above it all and always approached their children with gentle patience, while the "lion" parents stalked their children and approached them with aggression. We were told by the presenter we had to be "giraffe" parents who never used the word "no" to avoid causing irreparable damage to our children. I remember thinking of my three-year-old and bursting into tears. I thought I was a terrible parent and was convinced I was a "lion" who certainly had already damaged my sweet baby beyond repair because I wasn't always patient and I did occasionally say "no." What I didn't know then was, my daughter is on the Fetal Alcohol Spectrum and processes information in a radically different manner than her siblings. While I could spend time giving her siblings explanations, my daughter didn't understand my long and surely insightful reasoning and instead needed concise and consistent messages she could understand.

One of the ways in which my child's and many other children's information processing challenges become evident is when they are given directions. I have the distinct memory of my daughter and her same-aged brother sitting on the stairs putting their shoes on. It was a typical day for the parent of three under the age of four, and I was busily giving them directions to get their shoes and coats on so we could go to the park. I remember in the time my daughter was able to get her shoes on her brother had his shoes and coat on and was waiting at the door in anticipation of a trip to the park. I finished helping my daughter get her coat on, but when I opened the door she fell apart at the thought of going to the park. She was thoroughly upset because in her world no one had bothered to tell her we were leaving the house. Her same-aged brother and older sister had gotten the message that we were getting ready so we could go to the park, but my daughter had only gotten the message to put her shoes on and was completely blindsided by the fact we were going to the park. These meltdowns happened on a daily and sometimes hourly basis until I finally understood she wasn't "getting" what I was saying.

The issue wasn't that I was a "giraffe" or "lion" parent or that she was a willful and disobedient child—rather the issue was my daughter couldn't process the information quickly enough to catch up with a multi-step instruction. If I was giving a three-step instruction such as, "Put on your shoes and coat and let's get ready to go to the park," she might get one of those steps but not the other two, and she might get the middle or last step but not the first, and be totally confused as to why everyone was frustrated that she wasn't moving along with the rest of the group.

In my work I also see this miscue time and time again: children moving at a different pace than their parents, siblings and friends and everyone ending up frustrated because they don't understand what the other is doing or needing. When working with children who have been prenatally exposed to toxins I encourage parents to follow eight simples "rules" laid out by the National Organization on Fetal Alcohol Syndrome:

- Concrete

- Consistency

- Repetition

- Routine

- Simplicity

- Specific

- Structure

- Supervision.

Our kids need more time to learn, even if it means doing it over and over and over again.

Children who have been prenatally exposed to toxins also often struggle with inflexible thinking; they want to read the same story over and over again in exactly the same way. If plans change they often fall apart. They seem unable to "go with the flow." Playing games is a great way to help kids learn to be more flexible in their thinking in a fun and less demanding way.

This brings me to the idea of finding the "sweet spot" of game playing. You want game playing to be fun and to build attachment. Plus, it is a great way to challenge kiddos who struggle with inflexible thinking by making subtle and intentional changes to the game as time goes on. As they learn one skill, you add another.

What do I mean by the "sweet spot"? I mean the balance between playing because it is fun and playing with intention in a way that helps your child gain more skills and confidence. Finding the "sweet spot" requires the parent to be acutely in tune with their child. Because of this need to be in tune with your child, here are some suggestions before you start your game:

1. Choose a time to play when you and your child can commit 100 percent of your attention to each other. Don't attempt to squeeze a game in while you are trying to get dinner on the table or helping another sibling with their homework. Choose a time when you are both calm and available.

2. Choose a game that suits the mood of the day. For instance, one day your child might express an interest in cooking and you could play the "Family cookbook" game; or they may have been talking about family and you decide to play the "Family photo puzzle" game.

3. Have games ready in advance. Many of the games in this book require some materials and set-up. Make sure you have done this in advance of suggesting a game. There is nothing worse than having buy-in from your child to play a game, only to discover you don't have what you need to play it.

4. Finally, make sure you pay attention to how your child is "feeling." If your child is becoming frustrated with the game, ask them what they need and offer to change the game to make it more enjoyable; or if they seem to have mastered a skill you can adapt the game to increase their tolerance of change—but only if they seem to tolerate the change. Remember, playing games is about bonding and fun, it is not about playing the game "right" or pushing your child to do something that makes them uncomfortable.

The most important thing is, have fun together!

BACK DRAWINGS

(CONNECTING THE TWO OF YOU)

Age: 5 and up

Play time: This is dependent on the child. You may need to start out with one minute and build up to longer periods of time, depending on the child's reaction to touch.

Pacing (finding the "sweet spot")

In this game it is essential to remember that children who have been prenatally exposed to drugs and/or alcohol may have sensory issues, such that they may find touch calming or it may set their teeth on edge. They may need light, quick touch or they may need firm, constant touch. Some kids may run in for a quick hug and that is enough, while some kids may need to be held for 15 minutes.

Before beginning this game be sure you know what kind of touch your child enjoys and how long they can tolerate touch. You can even ask your child something like, "Today I thought we could play the back drawings game. Would you like me to draw on your back or your hand? Do you want me to draw with just my finger or my whole hand?" If this seems too complicated for your child you can show them the different touches and ask which one they would prefer. If in the middle of the game they begin to squirm or show other signs of discomfiture, check in with them and see if they need to stop, or if they want a turn to draw letters on you, or if they would like a different kind of touch.

You'll know you have found the "sweet spot" if your child giggles in delight, becomes completely relaxed and/or is engaged in deciphering the shapes you are making. You want your child to associate this game with positive feelings of touch, so never force them to stay in the game if it becomes frustrating or uncomfortable for them.

As Daniel Hughes and Jonathan Baylin (2012, p.35) state in their book *Brain-Based Parenting: The Neuroscience of Caregiving for Healthy Attachment*. "Once the dopamine system learns about a good thing, it stores a memory of it and then fires in anticipation of having that rewarding experience again."[4] Through this game children will learn touch can be fun and loving and will begin to anticipate the fun of back drawings and spending time with their parents. They will also begin to anticipate and associate learning with fun and caring.

This is a great game for helping a child learn about safe, nurturing touch, not only in the context of someone touching them, but also in the context of them touching someone else. For many children who have been exposed to drugs and alcohol during pregnancy, their sense of "body space" may not coincide with that of those around them. They may intrude into another person's space and not be aware of what they are doing, or they may want to be close but not like to be touched.

When playing this game with a child who may have sensory and or "body space" issues, they may need some cues from parents to help them understand where their body is in relationship to someone else and how they can be close without being touched if it is too uncomfortable.

How to play

When inviting a child to sit in front of the parent, if necessary the parent can cue the child as to where their body is. For example, the parent asks the child to sit in front of them with their back touching the parent's knees, but when the child sits down they are on the parent's lap. The parent can redirect the child by saying, "Do you notice where your body is? Is it in front of my knees or on my knees?" This helps the child to become more aware of where their body is in relationship to those around them. If the child sits too far away for the parent to comfortably reach the child, the parent might say, "Wow, you sat too far away from me. Could you come closer?"

If it seems the child does not want to be touched, the parent can encourage the child to just sit next to them. They can ask the child, "Can I draw one line on your back?" If even this seems too much, the parent can ask if they can put a hand on the child's back. Some children need firm touch rather than light touch, so making animal shapes out of whole hands may work better. The idea is to begin where the child is comfortable and build upon that.

---

4   Hughes, D. and Baylin, J. (2012) *Brain-based Parenting: The Neuroscience of Caregiving for Healthy Attachment.* London and New York: W.W. Norton and Company. p.35.

When asking if the child wants to draw on the parent's back, the same cuing can be used. If the child is too close: "Wow, it seems like it would be hard to draw when you are that close." Also, if the child draws too hard the parent needs to redirect the child and be sure they can draw on the parent's back without inflicting pain.

Optional

The parent can use this time to talk about letters and animals and begin to help the child relate letters to sounds and words. Many children who have been exposed to drugs and alcohol in utero have a very low frustration threshold, and this game is a good way to introduce learning in a non-threatening and loving way.

FAMILY COOKBOOK

(CONNECTING THE WHOLE FAMILY)

Age: 5 and up
Play time: varies

For children who have food issues or who have a difficult time following verbal directions, creating a cookbook can be a great way to get them to try new foods. When children are involved in the preparation of food, they are much more likely to try it, even if it is something they think they don't like. Using pictures instead of words in the cookbook enables the child to play a greater part in the preparation of food.

Pacing (finding the "sweet spot")

In this game it is essential to remember children who have been prenatally exposed to drugs and/or alcohol may have difficulty with memory and/or following multi-step instructions. Finding the "sweet spot" in this game requires parents to gauge their child's ability and not overwhelm them, while allowing them some room to gain independence with cooking. Cooking is an essential skill your child will need for the rest of his or her life.

This game may take quite a bit of set-up, depending on the needs of your child. If your child knows which food is which, you may not need to take pictures of individual ingredients. However, if your child has difficulty recalling the difference between butter and peanut butter, food pictures will come in handy. You can decide in advance which recipes you are going to cook and take pictures of all the ingredients to make a "food directory" with laminated pictures of lots of different foods.

For this game, the parent and child can decide together which recipe to make. However, keeping in mind the "sweet spot," you may want to give your child only two opinions, making sure you have the ingredients before you offer a particular choice. (Say, the choice is between peanut butter and honey sandwiches and cheese toast.) You and your child can find the pictures of the ingredients together, your child can find the actual ingredients (with help from the pictures) and you can make the recipe together.

You can even add a little more fun to the game by using cookie cutters to cut the sandwiches into fun shapes. Remember, the game is about fun and attachment, not eating your crusts!

How to play

Follow the directions given in Chapter 4 (see pages 93–94), but pare the number of recipes down to five or so simple family favorites (more can always be added later). Start with simple recipes like peanut butter and jelly sandwiches, with a twist such as cutting the sandwiches into triangles. This will allow children to gain mastery of a few simple steps.

Parent and child can take pictures of preparation to include in the book. For example, if the recipe calls for one cup of cheese, take a picture of the measuring cup full of cheese. This will help the child know which measuring cup to use, as well as what goes in the cup. Make this fun and involve the entire family as much as possible; children love to cook even though it is messy.

Comments on the game

The cookbook can be used to prompt children about the names of food and how much is needed. If the recipe calls for three eggs, the child and parent can find the eggs together and count the number needed. This game can also help your child to gain confidence and mastery of everyday living skills such as cooking and cleaning up. This helps children learn while engaged in a fun and bonding game with their parents.

Parents can add onto this game and include shopping for ingredients. Before going to the grocery store, the parent and child should make a list and discuss what they are going to buy; having a plan is always helpful in order to avoid a grocery store meltdown. Shopping for a few simple items can help children learn about using a grocery store and money. If you take pictures of where items are found in the store, children will begin to learn how to navigate their way in a store.

SCRIBBLE

(CONNECTING THE TWO OF YOU)

Age: 5 and up

Play time: varies: dependent on child. Start out slow and build up length of play time.

Pacing (finding the "sweet spot")

This is a great game to help children who have been prenatally exposed to drugs and/or alcohol work on letters and spelling in a non-threatening and playful way. Many children who have been exposed to drugs and/or alcohol will need more direction from a parent. For many of these children, it is difficult for them to organize their play independently and they often benefit from gentle, patient and loving direction from a parent. You can gauge how much direction your child will need. If they become frustrated while trying to "scribble" the letters, you may want to try another game or decide to play this particular game on another day.

How to play

The parent and child decide to "scribble" the alphabet together. For instance, the parent can say, "Let's draw the letter A together." The parent or child can start with the first line and each person can "draw" parts of the letter A. The parent may want to have an example board of the alphabet for the child to reference as they draw.

Some children may become frustrated when playing this game as they may have difficulty in drawing the letters correctly. You may want to start the game very slowly and play for only a minute or two, increasing the length of time you play each time. During the child's turn to draw, the parent does not correct or make changes to the child's drawing. However, when it is the parent's turn to draw, the parent may choose to draw the letter correctly. For example, a child may draw the letter "f" instead of the letter "t." The parent does not correct the child when it is the child's turn. Rather, the parent waits until it is their turn to draw the letter "t" correctly. The goal is to spend time together and enjoy one another with a little learning on the side.

For younger children, the parent can start by drawing shapes rather than letters. You can also use different colors and help the child learn their colors. This game requires the parent to be more intentional in their playing, while still allowing the child to lead the game.

Optional

If the child gets really good at this game you can add another element of learning and begin with, "What sound does the letter A make?" and later, "What animal names begin with the letter A?" Again, we don't want the child to become frustrated; rather you want them to trust you will help them learn in a loving and fun environment.

THE COLOR OF FEELINGS

(CONNECTING THE WHOLE FAMILY)

Age: 5 and up

Play time: varies

Pacing (finding the "sweet spot")

For many children, naming their feelings is difficult at best and more often it is impossible. Children may know they are sad or mad but may not know the names of those feelings or what to do with them when they experience them. This game is a good way for children to begin to recognize and name their feelings, as well as understand that everyone shares the same feelings, and that they shouldn't be afraid or ashamed of their feelings.

Children who have been prenatally exposed to drugs and/or alcohol often have a difficult time with executive functioning, the part of the brain which allows most of us to continue functioning without experiencing a meltdown every time we feel a feeling. Anyone who has witnessed a two-year-old's meltdown in the middle of a grocery store when they are told they can't have an ice cream has witnessed a deficit of executive functioning.

As children learn to recognize and name their emotions, they learn to have more control over them. If a child can begin to understand that when they are feeling anger it starts in their stomach and works its way down to their clenched hands, they can begin to control the anger and all being well, talk about it.

Pacing is very important in this game, as children can easily become overwhelmed when talking about feelings. They may need more direction, to go at a slower pace, and/or more opportunities to take breaks (they may want to draw dinosaurs or flowers in the middle of talking about the color of sad). This is completely normal, and it is important for the parent to follow the child's lead. This can be a project you come back to time and time again.

How to play

You will need to purchase large pieces of butcher paper. Each family member can lie on a piece of paper and another family member traces the outline of his or her body. This game can be scaled down to use regular-sized paper if the family does not have access to large body-sized pieces of paper. Instead of tracing the outline of a body, they can draw a body on a smaller piece of paper. You will also need colored paper cut into small pieces; any shape will do. (See Figure 7.2).

The parent can begin the game by saying something like, "I think happy is the color yellow and when I feel happy I feel it in my face." The parent then places a piece of yellow paper on the face of their body. Each family member can take a turn naming a feeling, the color they associate with the feeling, and where on the body they feel it. Some children may need a little prompting, such as, "I see you choose black for your mad feeling, where do you feel it when you are mad?"

Comments on the game

Children will enjoy seeing that their parents also feel mad, sad and happy. This can help children feel not so alone in their feelings and can help them to join in the family's feelings as well. This game can also help children begin to recognize when feelings are coming up, and they may begin to notice, for example, that when they are angry their mouth becomes dry, or their hands clench. As children begin to recognize feelings and how they begin, they can gain more control over them.

Figure 7.2: The color of feelings

THIS LITTLE PIGGY

(CONNECTING THE TWO OF YOU)

Age: Infant/Toddler/School age
Play time: Dependent on child and their attention span

Pacing (finding the "sweet spot")

For many children who have been exposed prenatally to drugs and/ or alcohol, learning and retaining information may be challenging and variable. While their peers are catching onto and being successful at games such as, "Where's your nose?" and "This little piggy," children who have been prenatally exposed to drugs and/or alcohol may be able to tell you where their nose is one day and not the next, or not at all.

Games like, "This little piggy" and "Where's your nose?" can be used to connect parent and child, as well as being fun learning tools. Children love repetition and playing these games over and over again not only delights them but can help them to learn where their body parts are and the names of those body parts.

Remember to pace the game in time with your child. If they are having a particularly challenging game then you might want to simply play the game by saying something like, "here is your nose and here is my nose." If they are having a day in which they seem up for a challenge you can encourage them to play the little piggy game and find their own body parts, and then your body parts. If they seem to need some help, you can name the body part first and then have your child name the body part. If they can't seem to remember any of their body parts or aren't in a mood to play the game you can hold them in your arms or in your lap and gently name body parts for them. As the child's system starts to "wake up" you may notice him or her begin to name things on their own.

How to play

The parent and child play these games normally but with a little more focus on learning about body parts. The child will delight in playing with you and won't notice the intention of repetition, in fact, they will delight in being able to master finding their piggies, nose and eyes.

Once they have learned the names of their body parts you can move onto helping them learn your body parts. Some children who have been affected by exposure to drugs and alcohol have a very difficult time with generalization. So, while they may master finding their body parts it may be difficult for them to generalize that knowledge to others. Yes, they know where their piggies are but can they find where your piggies are? Can they find them when you have shoes on, when you just have socks on, when they are bare? Can they find the dog's piggies or their sister's piggies?

Again, children delight in repetition and just being close to their parent. Repetition helps the brain to get moving and building very important neural pathways. This game can also be played if a child has difficulty "getting going" in the morning or after a nap. The parent can play this game to help the child get moving slowly and gently.

FAMILY PHOTO PUZZLE

(CONNECTING THE WHOLE FAMILY)

Age: 5 and up
Play time: 30 minutes

This family jigsaw puzzle is a great way to help children who may feel disconnected from their family to feel more connected by learning who various family members are and working to build a picture of their family.

Children love to look at pictures. For children who may have difficulty retaining who the many members of their family are and/or who get anxious when they are away from their family, creating a family puzzle they can carry with them and put together over and over again will help them remember family members and give them the security of being able to look at pictures of their family when they are away.

Pacing (finding the "sweet spot")

For many children who have been exposed prenatally to drugs and/ or alcohol recall can be very challenging. They may easily be able to recall the members of their immediate family, but have more difficulty recalling grandparents, aunts, uncles etc. This can be distressing for not only your child but for family members as well.

In this game you want to make sure you are following your child's lead by not introducing too much information for them to process. You may want to start out by making a puzzle of your nuclear family, even if there are just two of you, this is a good place to start. You can add more people to the "puzzle" as your child is able to recall each puzzle piece (person), or as your child requests to add more pieces.

This is a game your child will love to play over and over again. Not only will they love looking at pictures of their family and talking about different people but it also help build their recall capacity.

How to play

Follow the directions given for this game earlier in the book, however, for children who have difficulty retaining information, you will want to begin with just a few pictures of their primary family members, i.e., parents, siblings and grandparents. Also, large pieces with fewer edges may be easier for children who struggle with fine motor skills and putting things together. As the child gains mastery you can create smaller and more challenging pieces.

Optional

For children who are struggling with the loss of their birth family, you can also create a puzzle using any pictures of their birth family you may have.

Comments on the game

This is a great game for the entire family to be involved in. Each family member can choose one to two pictures depending on the size of the family and talk about why they chose a certain picture, and tell a family story about it. This not only aids in family bonding but also provides a wonderful opportunity for children to hear family stories. For children who have been exposed to drugs and/or alcohol, the repetition of telling family stories helps them to remember those stories as well as attach positive feelings to them.

Figure 7.3: Family photo puzzle

Figure 7.4: Family photo puzzle

Figure 7.5: Family photo puzzle

Addendum

Notes for Professionals

BY JILL DZIKO

As professionals we constantly look for new and more effective ways of working with our clients. We read books. We attend consultation groups and continuing education classes. We talk with colleagues. We wake up in the middle of the night worrying that we don't have enough "expertise" to work with a certain client. We do all of these things in the pursuit of excellence. So, you may be asking yourself, "How can a book of games help the children in my practice?" Well, I believe game playing is one of the best ways to learn about life. Games can help children improve their executive functioning and learn to be more flexible in their thinking. Games can help families improve their attachment with one another. They can also teach children and families about relationships and each other. Most important of all, games can help families have fun together!

I know for many of the families I work with, joy and fun have given way to day-to-day drudgery. Parents are not having fun as they spend hours trying to find the right services for their children, and often become resentful when parenting is not what they expected. Children are not having fun as they struggle in school and with peers. They then often come home to parents who are tired and stressed out. By the time I see families, they have often forgotten what it is to enjoy each other and simply have fun together.

This book of games is a great way to remind and help families to have fun together—to give them a prescription, if you will, for taking time each and every day to just play together. To commit five to 20 minutes of every day (if they can't, then at least every week) in the pursuit of having fun together.

I have seen this idea of having fun change families. I often assign "homework" to the families I work with and the "homework" is usually to pick one activity a week when they have fun together. They must agree to turn off all phones, TVs and computers, and choose a fun activity in which everyone participates. Sometimes it is as simple as watching a movie together, or as complex as bowling and dinner. The idea is to help families rediscover what they love and enjoy about each other and to give themselves permission to have fun in this overloaded world we all live in.

This book is a collection of games designed to bring families together to build attachment. It can also be used in the professional setting, with many of the games easily adaptable for this purpose. I find it helpful to have suggestions from other professionals to fall back on when things just don't go the way I planned during a session.

I remember working with an adolescent boy and my plan was to talk with him about racial identity. The session began with our usual discussion of lacrosse and his upcoming games, but when I tried to move the conversation toward race and racial identity my normally engaging and verbose client went completely silent and my mind went blank! Fortunately, sitting on my table was a drawing book created by social workers who work with terminally ill kids (and a great book for every kid). I picked up the book, handed it to my client, and as he began drawing and filling in the questions in the book, the conversation once again began to flow. I was so thankful to have the help of someone else's words. I hope this book of games can be that help for other professionals. When you are in need of ideas in your office or for families who are struggling, I hope this book will be a resource and source of support.

BY JULIE FISHER

My name is Julie Fisher and I am a Licensed Clinical Social Worker. I work at Kindering, a birth-to-three early intervention center in Bellevue, Washington. For more than a decade my clinical work has been with foster families and their children. The program I am a part of, CHERISH™ (**CH**ildren **E**ncouraged by **R**elationships **I**n **S**ecure **H**omes), is an infant mental health home-visiting program whose mission is to help foster children and their foster parents or relative caregivers form secure attachments.

Working with children from birth to three is a hopeful endeavor. Thanks to neuroplasticity, these first years in a child's life are the most critical, as during this stage of development the brain is at its most receptive and adaptable. The majority of infants who come into foster care have been prenatally exposed to substances; many foster children's developmental delays stem from this substance exposure, along with the trauma of experiencing abuse and neglect. Compounding these insults are the grief and loss that come with having multiple homes and attachment figures. During these early years, developmental delays are not always detected by standardized tests. Therefore it is crucial to have an early intervention workforce that is trained in assessing attachment disruptions and regulation concerns. My passion has been bringing the concept of infant mental health more centrally into the field of early intervention.

Because of the Child Abuse and Prevention Treatment Act (CAPTA, originally written in 1974, and reauthorized several times, most recently in 2010), foster children must be screened for developmental delays. Thus, the early intervention system is an ideal place for identifying early needs and a natural location for housing infant mental health services.

In early intervention, five areas of development are assessed: speech and language; cognitive, motor, adaptive, and social and emotional development. To strengthen social and emotional development, we focus on attachment. All early learning occurs in primary attachment relationships. When trust and security are lacking, it is hard to make progress in other areas of development; and conversely, these other areas of development greatly impact on how children connect to their birth or adoptive parents or primary caregivers. The benefits of having an interdisciplinary team to treat young foster children cannot be overstated.

How do babies and toddlers securely attach to their caregivers? Attachment security happens when a baby's cues are read correctly and her needs are met. With this happening repeatedly, there is a process of falling in love that takes place between baby and caregiver. One way we know attachment security is forming is through the experience of delight. "Delighting in" is one of the concepts used in the Circle of Security, a well-known attachment curriculum. When a parent delights in a child, the heart is joyful simply because that child exists. Children need to have someone who feels this way about them.

The games in this book are to help parents and children play together to increase this "delighting in." They are tools on the path to more attachment security and self-regulation. Children gain self-regulation through being in relationship with a parent who is well-regulated. They borrow from parental regulation in order to build their own. Since it can be extremely difficult to parent children who have minimal self-regulation skills, much of my therapy focuses on parental well-being. Just like the oxygen mask on the airplane, parental survival depends on addressing parental self-care.

One way to increase parental self-regulation is for parents to practice mindfulness; and since this work is a parallel process, professionals helping parents also need to practice mindfulness. Being mindful means letting go of the past and the future; as those only exist as concepts in the present. Children function in the present and need their parents to be there, too. Fortunately, this being present, or attuned, has been researched and only needs to happen for children about 30 percent of the time.[5] This is good news! The things that compete for parental attention are varied and vast, making it very hard to stay present.

As therapists, educators, and parents, it is sustaining to have a mindfulness practice, such as meditation, journaling, or yoga. Knowing you have a daily break from the business of life, a chance to step off the hamster wheel, can make all the difference, and for professionals it is additionally crucial to spend time reflecting on our roles serving children and their parents with a supervisor or in a consultation group. Children depend on the self-regulation of the adults in their lives. *How* we are really, really matters. Thank you for being in the moment and staying hopeful.

5   Gray, D.D. (2014) "Close Connection." In *Attaching Through Love, Hugs, and Play*. London and Philadelphia, PA: Jessica Kingsley Publishers. p.53.

BY LAURA STONE

My name is Laura Stone and I am a Licensed Mental Health Counselor with a private practice in Seattle, Washington. My clients include adopted kids of all ages and their families. Often families come to see me who are seeking more connection with kids who have been through a rough or complicated beginning in life. The concept of stable family life, or even of "family," may be new to these kids, and their parents need help to get the process of attachment going in the right direction. Many kids arrive with behaviors that are hard to understand and make attachment more challenging. I work with parents first to make sense of risk factors and problematic behaviors, and to develop successful parenting strategies. I then work with parents and children together to get kids on track for attaching by mitigating barriers that get in the way, processing trauma and loss, forming solid identity, and developing relational skills.

In working with adoptive families and their young children I have found that nondirective, child-centered play therapy has limited value, at least in the beginning stages; often kids don't have much in their history that has developed their reflective capacity, so instead of processing through unstructured play in therapy they may replay aspects of their trauma repeatedly without much resolution. Approaches that rely on children to recognize and describe their thoughts and feelings can be similarly unproductive in getting started. Kids with complicated backgrounds (drug exposure, abuse, neglect, multiple change of caregivers) face obstacles to normal development and attachment because they have often missed out on fundamental early experiences, and in some cases have faced overwhelming adversity later in childhood. Instead of learning to trust, they experience periods of prolonged stress and their developing brains become wired under those conditions. Before they can really connect with others, these kids often need help to calm their systems.

A more directed approach that utilizes structured play, including games, seems to be a more successful way to embark in therapy. The beginning work with children involves teaching tools and skills for emotional regulation, helping children learn how to relax deeply, to recognize and connect with a parent's eyes and facial expressions, to receive soothing and mirroring, and to play in a relaxed and collaborative manner. Baby and toddler games, silly songs, soothing forms of art-making—activities lots of children didn't get in their earliest years—are ways to do some *rewiring* in the brain. Games and activities played with family create a sense of structure and safety and can teach kids *how to play*, how to relax the need for control, and how to tolerate feelings.

Foster and adoptive parenting can be overwhelmingly stressful, and attachment takes energy; for parents games are a way to remember, or learn, how to have fun with their children. When parents can find joy in being with their children they are less stressed and more likely to naturally do the things that encourage attachment, instead of trying too hard or becoming rigid or anxious in their approach.

As children engage further in the therapy process, and begin to sort through their personal narrative, much of the work focuses on challenging false perceptions about why things happened the way they did, and helping kids realize they aren't to blame for their relinquishment or their trauma. Having parents in the room and actively part of this work is pivotal in developing children's internal dialogue, what they will remember and tell themselves in the future, about their life story. I sometimes have kids and parents play games or activities made up on the spot after intense work in order to help kids practice with new ideas and self-talk, as well as ways of relating and speaking to others. The structure of the game or activity done at this point is containing and helps kids stay grounded as they hold new concepts in mind. At home, too, after periods of distress or discord between parents and children, games and calming activities are a means to come back together and affirm safety and connection.

I would advise professionals to recognize the importance of acquiring high-quality trauma and attachment-informed training before working with foster and adopted children and families. I would also encourage professionals to realize the value of seeing families, especially families with young children, together. Children develop in relationship with parents and so it follows, in my experience, that kids heal best in therapy in relationship with parent(s). Childhood is short and attachment is fundamental. Therapy can be powerful for young children, but in order to be effective in the long term, it needs to be directed at helping kids create sustainable, close, and supportive relationships with their parents.

Biographies

MEGAN CLARKE

Megan Clarke is a licensed marriage and family therapist in private practice in Bellevue, Washington. She holds a Bachelor of Arts in Communication from the University of Washington and a Masters Degree in Clinical Psychology from Antioch University, Seattle. She is also certified in trauma and attachment-focused therapy, as well as therapy with adoptive and foster families. Megan works with children, teens and adults with histories of trauma. She lives in Bellevue, Washington with her husband, two sons and golden retriever.

JILL DZIKO

Jill holds a Masters in Social Work from the University of Washington and is a licensed clinical social worker in Washington State. She has worked in the field of adoption for over 13 years and is certified in trauma-attachment focused therapy, as well as therapy with adoptive and foster families. She is currently the executive director of Your Adoptive Family, a non-profit licensed adoption agency she started in 2011. Jill is also the very proud parent of four wonderful children, three of whom were adopted at birth.

JULIE FISHER

Julie Fisher is a licensed clinical social worker who obtained her Masters in Social Work from the University of Washington. She has worked with foster children and their families since 2001, most recently as part of the CHERISH Program at Kindering in Bellevue, Washington. She currently trains other therapists on providing infant mental health services in early intervention settings. She lives with her husband, two children, and their dog in Shoreline, Washington.

DEBORAH GRAY

Deborah Gray specializes in the attachment, grief, and trauma issues of children in her practice, Nurturing Attachments. Her passion is to help families develop close, satisfying relationships. As a clinical social worker, she has worked over 25 years in foster and adopted children's therapies and placement. She has also been a therapeutic foster parent.

Deborah is core faculty for the award-winning postgraduate certificate program in Foster and Adoption Therapy at Portland State University. She is main faculty in the ATTACh-recognized postgraduate Attachment Therapy certificate program through Cascadia Training. She has taught in the Trauma certificate program at the University of Washington and was the 2008 Henry W. Maier Practitioner in Residence at the School of Social Work at the University of Washington.

Deborah Gray is a popular presenter due to her practical and positive approaches. She has keynoted conferences ranging from the Joint Council of International Children's Services to orphan conferences. She continues to work in a clinical practice with parents and children, who help to teach her new approaches and techniques every day. Visit her website at www.deborahdgray.com.

LAURA STONE

Laura Stone is a Licensed Mental Health Counselor with a private practice in the Queen Anne neighborhood of Seattle. She holds a Master's Degree in Psychology from Antioch University, as well as certificates in Adoption and Foster Care Therapy and Attachment-Trauma Focused Therapy. She has practiced professionally as a psychotherapist for over 15 years, both in agency settings and in private practice. Her clients include children, adolescents, adults, and families, most of whom have foster care and/or adoption as part of their story. She lives in Seattle with her husband and two children.

Resource List

Association for Treatment and Training in the Attachment of Children (ATTACh)

www.attach.org

This international organization helps parents and therapists when children are having significant difficulties with attachment. It publishes a "white paper" position on which therapies are considered helpful, and which are coercive and probably harmful.

BeeVisual, LLC

beevisual.com

This is a website with apps that help children to get and stay organized, and to learn and use social skills. Children are able to use tablets, phones, or computers with the applications.

Center on the Developing Child, Harvard University

www.developingchild.harvard.edu

This website contains informative reports, working papers, briefs, and videos on topics such as brain development, toxic stress, and executive function.

ChildTrauma Academy

Feigin Center, Suite 715
Texas Children's Hospital
6621 Fannin
Houston, TX 77030
www.childtrauma.org

This is an educational series for parents and caregivers. Bruce Perry, MD, Ph.D. composes or edits materials. Material is practical and accurate. It gives parents access to work from some of the finest caliber professionals.

Circle of Security International

Early intervention program for parents and children
www.circleofsecurity.net

The Circle of Security website offers information about their intervention program, training for parents and professionals, and free resource handouts that are downloadable. They also have a video that explains the Circle of Security graphic.

Center for Cognitive-Behavioral Assessment and Remediation

www.bgcenter.com

This is a website run by developmental psychologist Dr. Boris Gindis. It has many articles useful for educational planning, not exclusive to those adopted from Eastern Europe.

Children and Adults with Attention Deficit Disorder (CHADD)

8181 Professional Place, Suite 201
Landover, MD 20785
800-233-4050
301-306-7070
Fax: 301-306-7090
www.chadd.org

This organization is a powerhouse with information about education, medication, home routines, counseling, and local support groups. Invaluable in giving information to advocate for school planning.

Child Information Gateway

www.childwelfare.gov

Child Welfare Information Gateway provides access to information and resources to help protect children and strengthen families. Provides information about all aspects of adoption and about child abuse and neglect. Includes publications, referrals to services, and searches of its computerized information databases. A service of the Children's Bureau, Administration for Children and Families, US Department of Health and Human Services.

Families Moving Forward

http://depts.washington.edu/fmffasd

This is a program that is designed to help children with Fetal Alcohol Spectrum Disorder (FASD) and their families. The FMF program has been offered as a home visiting intervention model, but these intervention techniques can likely also be used in mental health clinics, early intervention settings, child guidance centers, or in settings where FASD diagnosis is done.

Fostering Families Today

www.fosteringfamiliestoday.com

The magazine, published by Louis and Co (who also publish *Adoption Today*), is packed with sound and well-written articles, and is graphically attractive as well. It is also helpful for later-placed adopted children. It is one of my favorite resources in the field.

Friends of Russian and Ukrainian Adoption and Neighboring Countries (FRUA)

PO Box 2944
Merrifield, VA 22116
www.frua.org

This organization is a powerhouse. Join and sign up for their *Family Focus* newsletter and make use of their dynamic online discussion group. Better yet, go to, or order tapes from their national conference. You do not have to have adopted a child from Eastern Europe in order to appreciate these resources.

Institute of Child Development, Texas Christian University

www.child.tcu.edu

This is a great resource for parents. Inspired by Dr. Karyn Purvis and Dr. David Cross, the website sells DVDs, displays trainings, and provides educational resources of high quality. Many of the excellent trainings are free or of reduced cost.

Kinship Center

kinshipcenter.org

This is a great source for adoption-related information. Sharon Kaplan Rosia and her colleagues are the inspiration behind these materials, covering important aspects of parenting and professional support.

Model Me Kids

modelmekids.com

This is a website that sells DVDs for children who are learning social skills. It is great as a teaching tool for families or for schools. It is suitable for children after neglect or for children with autism.

National Child Traumatic Stress Network

nctsn.org

This is an excellent group with support for foster or adoptive parents who are parenting children who were traumatized. The website is excellent: parent-friendly for parents, practice-rich for therapists accessing it.

National Council on Adoptable Children (NACAC)

970 Raymond Avenue, Suite 106
St. Paul, MN 55114-1149
1-800-470-6665
www.nacac.org

This organization has legal, ethical, and practice influences on children's adoption issues. It is a powerful advocacy organization and leads in improving adoption practices.

Nuturing Attachments

www.nuturingattachments.com

This website, begun by Deborah Gray, has downloadable information for both parents and professionals. There is a forum for professionals who are treating families. It includes videos on a variety of issues important to foster or adoptive parents. While begun by Deborah Gray, it is designed to include the expertise and voices of many professionals and parents.

Pact, an Adoption Alliance

3450 Sacramento Street, Suite 239
San Francisco, CA 94118
425-221-6957
Fax: 510-482-2089
www.pactadopt.org

An adoption placement and education service focused on placing children of color and supporting families raising adopted children of color either in-racially or transracially

Sensory Processing Disorders

www.sensory-processing-disorder.com

This is a great website for parents whose children may have sensory sensitivities. It has a checklist and a series of actions to take to help your child.

Sibshops

www.siblingsupport.org

The sibling support project has developed an international directory of these workshops designed to best support siblings of children with special needs. The kids love them.

Society of Special Needs Adoptive Parents (SNAP) newsletter

604.687.3364
snap@snap.bc.ca

This provides the latest on special needs issues, including Fetal Alcohol Spectrum Disorder (FASD). It is extremely practical. SNAP also has a great downloadable book on parenting children affected by FASD.

BOOKS FOR ADULTS AND FOR CHILDREN

All About Adoption. Marc Nemiroll and Jane Annunziata. (Magination Press, 2004). This children's book for ages 6–11 includes good information about children's feelings, adoptive families, and birthparents. It covers anxiety, older child adoption, and birthparent issues.

Attaching Through Love, Hugs, and Play. Deborah D. Gray. (Jessica Kingsley Publishers, 2014). This practical book has photos to show parents the joyful process of attaching to their children. It includes typical behaviors that occur when children are highly stressed—as well as ways to help children. There is ample information on ways to help children when they struggle with organizing, getting the big picture, self-monitoring, or stopping impulses. The book includes a parent-friendly guide into the teen years. It concludes with a bonding and attachment assessment so that parents can track their progress.

Attaching in Adoption, Practical Tools for Today's Parents. Deborah Gray. (Jessica Kingsley Publishers, 2012). This book describes ways to promote attachment at every stage of a baby or child's development. It provides the reasons for some of the obstacles that parents and children face. It gives many practical approaches that help with connection as well as discipline. Parents will find sound parenting strategies adapted to the needs of fostered or adopted children. This book is a guide written specifically for families whose children need extra nurture and know-how.

Attachment in Common Sense and Doodles: A Practical Guide. Miriam Silver. (Jessica Kingsley Publishers, 2013). This book describes attachment issues in a clear, straightforward manner.

Attachment Play: How to Solve Children's Behavior Problems with Play, Laughter, and Connection. Aletha Solter, Ph.D. (Shining Star Press, 2013). Known for providing parents with discipline alternatives to "time out," Dr. Solter's most recent book is a helpful resource on the use of play to increase connections with children.

The Best Single Mom in the World: How I Was Adopted. Mary Zisk. (Albert Whitman and Company, 2001). Want a cheerfully illustrated read-aloud book for a single parent family? This is it.

Brain-Based Parenting: The Neuroscience of Caregiving for Healthy Attachment. Daniel A. Hughes and Jonathan Baylin. (W.W. Norton and Company, Inc 2012). A great book for understanding the neuroscience of attachment. Easy and enjoyable to read.

Building your Bounce: Simple Strategies for a Resilient You. (Second edition.) Mary Mackrain and Nefertiti Bruce with the Devereux Center for Resilient Children. (Kaplan, 2013). Concise booklet for parents that covers self-care and resilience. Designed to be used in conjunction with the Devereux Adult Resilience Survey (DARS), which is contained in the booklet and is available for free download online.

Calm-Down Time. Elizabeth Verdick. (Free Spirit Publishing, 2010). This book is a wonderful board book to share with toddlers. There are self-calming activities you can try together as you read.

Child with Special Needs: Encouraging Intellectual and Emotional Growth. Stanley Greenspan and Serena Wieder. (Addison Wesley, 1998.) Sophisticated parents or professionals will appreciate this approach, which stimulates development.

A Child's Journey Through Placement. Vera Fahlberg, M.D. (Jessica Kingsley Publishers, 2012.) This beautifully written book is a treasure for professionals who are placing children or raising children. Dr. Fahlberg's wisdom and sensitivity shine through.

The Connected Child. Karyn Purvis and David Cross. (McGraw-Hill, 2007). This is a valuable book for adoptive parents—especially those looking for some brain-based reasons why their children behave the way that they do. Dr. Purvis and Dr. Cross give excellent answers to parents who are looking for ways to raise more challenging children kindly, and yet with limits. This is a solid book by experienced professionals. They are warm, wise, and caring as they encourage parents.

Connecting with Kids Through Stories. Denise Lacher, Todd Nichols and Joanne May. (Jessica Kingsley Publishers, 2005). This book employs storytelling to help children to change their narratives and schema of life. It gives a helpful guide to parents and to clinicians.

Creating Capacity for Attachment. Arthur Becker-Weidman and Deborah Shell (eds.). (Wood and Barnes Publishing, 2005). This book is a lovely addition to the literature. It helps clinicians to develop their practice skills in areas of assessment, attunement, and treatment for children with attachment issues.

Creating Loving Attachments: Parenting with PACE to Nurture Confidence and Security in the Troubled Child. Kim Golding and Daniel Hughes. (Jessica Kingsley Publishers, 2012). I so enjoyed the emphasis on nurture and play in this book. The book is written for sophisticated parents, or parent professionals. It helps keep parents sensitive and communicative, and is especially good for children in late elementary years and up.

Delivered from Distraction: Getting the Most out of Life with Attention Deficit Disorder. Edward Hallowell and John Ratey. (Ballantine Books, 2005). This book is a guide for some many aspects of life. It is a great book for families with a member with ADD.

Even if I Did Something Awful? Barbara Shook Hazen. (Atheneum, 1981). A book to reassure younger children that they are loved, no matter what.

Executive Skills in Children and Adolescents. Peg Dawson and Richard Guare. (Guilford Press, 2010.) This is a workbook with templates that help your teen to plan and organize their school projects, their rooms, and their time. Invaluable!

Fostering Changes: Myth, Meaning and Magic Bullets in Attachment Theory. Richard Delaney. (Wood and Barnes Publishing, 2006.) This book describes good techniques and an updated theoretical base as a way to help older children in foster homes. The book is practical and respectful.

Growing an In-Sync Child. Carol Kranowitz. (Perigee Press, 2010). This is another practical book that helps children move beyond the limits of sensory sensitivities. This is the latest, following *The Out of Sync Child* and *The Out of Sync Child Has Fun,* which demystified sensory sensitivities and how to parent a child who has them.

Healing Parents: Helping Wounded Children Learn to Trust and Love. Michael Orlans and Terry M. Levy. (Child Welfare League of America, Inc., 2006). This is a wonderful book filled with information about attachment and ways parents can help their children heal through their relationship.

Helping Adolescents with ADHD and Learning Disabilities: Ready-to-Use Tips, Techniques, and Checklists for School Success. Judith Greenbaum Ph.D., Geraldine Markel Ph.D. (Jossey-Bass, 2001.) This book is great in giving ideas for IEPs and school meetings. It helps parents and teens in school matters.

Help is on the Way: A Child's Book About ADD. Marc Neniroff and Jane Annunziata. (Magination Press, 1998.) This is a fun and readable book to use with children who have been diagnosed with ADD.

Inside Transracial Adoption. Gail Steinberg and Beth Hall. (Jessica Kingsley Publishers, 2013.) This book explores the complexities of transracial adoption while equipping parents with practical and compassionate advice. To top it off, it is a good read!

Mental Health in Early Intervention: Achieving Unity in Principles and Practice. Gilbert Foley, Ed.D. and Jane Hochman, Ed.D. (eds.). (Brookes Publishing, 2006.) This professional development resource helps early intervention providers better understand infant mental health, and infant mental health providers better understand early intervention.

The Mindful Path to Self-compassion: Freeing Yourself from Destructive Thoughts and Emotions. Christopher K. Germer, Ph.D. (Guilford Press, 2009.) This book serves as a comprehensive guide on the topics of mindfulness and self-compassion.

The Mulberry Bird. Anne Braff Brodzinsky. (Jessica Kingsley Publishers, 2012). Children who are in elementary school like this book. It is particularly helpful to children who have a history of poor care. The children use metaphors to talk to parents.

The Mystery of Risk. Ira Chasnoff. (NTI Upstream, 2011.) This is a great book for parents whose children were prenatally exposed to alcohol and/or drugs. Ira Chasnoff gives clear information about brain functioning after exposure and how to bring out the best in children.

Navigating the Social World. Jeanette McAfee. (Future Horizons, 2002.) This is a handbook for children who have difficulty with social relatedness. It includes exercises to build these capacities in the older child. I have used this in a guided way with college-age coaches and my pre-teen clients, with excellent success.

No Bad Kids: Toddler Discipline Without Shame. Janet Lansbury. (JLML Press, 2014). This is a collection of practical articles written on toddler behaviors and respectful parenting practices.

No Mind Left Behind: Understanding and Fostering Executive Control. Adam Cox. (Perigee Press, 2008.) This is an outstanding book for parents who are developing executive functioning in their families. The book's tone is positive and the suggestions are solid.

Nurturing Adoptions: Creating Resilience after Neglect and Trauma. Deborah D. Gray. (Jessica Kingsley Publishers, 2012). This book provides guidance on methods to help children in the home and in therapy after neglect or trauma. It includes a guide for parents who are helping children through the grieving process. This book describes what trauma looks like at every stage of development—and what to do about it. For the professional and parent, the book includes schedules for moving children between homes so that they are not further traumatized. Professionals will find a home study template that assesses attachment. The book outlines classic cases in which attachment, neglect, and trauma have all been treated successfully.

Parenting Children Affected by Fetal Alcohol Syndrome: A Guide for Daily Living. Ministry for Children and Families, British Columbia). Available as a free downloaded book from snap@snap.bc.ca., regularly updated, and an extremely practical guide to daily schedules and an understanding of approaches that work with prenatally exposed infants, children, and teens.

Parenting from the Inside Out. Daniel J. Siegel and Mary Hartzell. (Penguin/Putnam, 2003.) This excellent book explores building family relationships in a brain-based, attachment-friendly, but warm manner.

Play: How it Shapes the Brain, Opens the Imagination, and Invigorates the Soul. Stuart Brown. (Penguin Group, 2009). This is an interesting book that details the many ways in which play not only enhances our lives but is essential to our happiness. Dr. Stuart Brown details his decades of research into play, and makes a strong case for incorporating play into all of our lives, children and adults alike!

Relationship Development Intervention with Children, Adolescents, and Adults. Steven E. Gutstein and Rachelle K. Sheely. (Jessica Kingsley Publishers, 2002) and *Relationship Development Intervention with Young Children.* Steven E. Gutstein and Rachelle K. Sheely. (Jessica Kingsley Publishers, 2002.) This book and the one above are the curricula for developing social skills. They are fantastic resources for schools and homes.

Self-Calming Cards. Elizabeth Crary and Mits Katayama. (Parenting Press, 2006.) This a deck of cards that show calming skills. Children aged 3–11 can pick out their favorite cards. They have easy visuals to show children what to do. The cards have Spanish or English words to match the pictures on the card.

Skills Training for Children with Behavioral Problems. (Revised edition.) Michael Bloomquist. (Guilford Press, 2006.) This is an excellent guide for parents and professionals who want tools, charts, and practical suggestions for reducing anger and anxiety through changes in thinking and reward systems. It helps the whole family with better self-control and helpful thoughts.

Taking Charge of ADHD. Russell A Barkley. (Guilford Press, 1995; revised 2005.) This author explains simply, but not superficially, what is going on with children with ADHD and what to do about it. Russell Barkley is not only a prolific writer and researcher, but also a caring advocate for children and their families.

Taking "No" for an Answer and Other Skills Children Need: 50 Games to Teach Family Skills. Laurie Simons. (Parenting Press, 2000.) This book is a great resource for helping families identify and change unhelpful patterns of interacting. Some of the games can be played with children as young as three.

Tell Me a Real Adoption Story, Betty Jean Lifton. (Alfred A. Knopf, 1993.) A book about a child's adoption story, to read together.

The Way I Feel. Janan Cain. (Parenting Press, 2005.) A tested favorite amongst young children for identifying feelings and practicing with a parent what those feelings look like on our faces.

Trauma Stewardship: An Everyday Guide to Caring for Self While Caring for Others. Laura Van Dernoot Lipsky with Connie Burk. (Berrett-Koehler Publishers, Inc., 2009.) A vital book regarding self-care and secondary trauma.

The Whole-Brain Child. Daniel Siegel and Tina Bryson. (Bantam Books, 2012.) This book helps parents to coach the development of better emotional control. It is full of strategies that reflect Dan Siegel's ongoing contributions in helping families with attachment and emotional regulation.

Understanding Myself: A Kid's Guide to Understanding Intense Emotions and Strong Feelings. Mary L. Lamia, Ph.D. (Magination Press, 2011.) A great resource for kids who need to make sense of their big feelings.

Welcoming a New Brother or Sister Through Adoption. Arleta James. (Jessica Kingsley Publishers, 2012.) This is a thorough, clear-headed look at adoption and the needs of all of the children in the family.

Zachery's New Home. Geraldine Blomquist and Paul Blomquist. (Magination Press, 1991.) The children's all-time favorite about beginning to trust after abuse.

Attaching Through Love, Hugs and Play
Simple Strategies to Help Build Connections with Your Child
Deborah D. Gray
Paperback: £12.99 / $19.95
ISBN: 978 1 84905 939 8
240 pages

Capturing the warmth and fun of forming close relationships with children, this book offers simple advice to parents of children who find it difficult to attach and bond – whether following adoption, divorce or other difficult experiences.

Attachment therapist Deborah D. Gray describes how to use the latest thinking on attachment in your daily parenting. She reveals sensory techniques which have proven to help children bond – straightforward activities like keeping close eye contact or stroking a child's feet or cheeks – and explains why routines like mealtimes and play time are so important in helping children to attach. The book offers positive ideas for responding to immediate crises like difficult behaviour and meltdowns, but importantly also offers longer-term strategies to help children to develop the skills they need to cope as they grow up – the ability to plan, concentrate and be in control of their emotions.

Offering fascinating insights into how children who struggle to attach can be helped, this book is full of easy-to-use ideas which will help you to enjoy the many pleasures of bonding and attaching with your child.

Deborah Gray, MSW, MPA specialises in the attachment, grief, and trauma issues of children in her practice, Nurturing Attachments. A clinical social worker, she has worked for over 25 years in foster and adopted children's therapies and placement. She is core faculty for the award-winning Post-Graduate Certificate program in Foster and Adoption Therapy at Portland State University and main faculty in the ATTACh-recognized Post-Graduate Attachment Therapy Certificate Program through Cascadia Training. She is the author of *Attaching Through Love, Hugs and Play: Simple Strategies to Help Build Connections with Your Child, Attaching in Adoption: Practical Tools for Today's Parents* and *Nurturing Adoptions: Creating Resilience after Neglect and Trauma*, also published by Jessica Kingsley Publishers. Visit her website at www.deborahdgray.com.

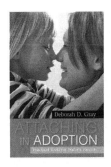

Attaching in Adoption
Practical Tools for Today's Parents
Deborah D. Gray
Paperback: £16.99 / $24.99
ISBN: 978 1 84905 890 2
400 pages

Attaching in Adoption is a comprehensive guide for prospective and actual adoptive parents on how to understand and care for their adopted child and promote healthy attachment.

This classic text provides practical parenting strategies designed to enhance children's happiness and emotional health. It explains what attachment is, how grief and trauma can affect children's emotional development, and how to improve attachment, respect, cooperation and trust. Parenting techniques are matched to children's emotional needs and stages, and checklists are included to help parents assess how their child is doing at each developmental stage. The book covers a wide range of issues including international adoption, Fetal Alcohol Spectrum Disorder, and learning disabilities, and combines sound theory and direct advice with case examples throughout.

This book is a must read for anyone interested in adoption and for all adoptive families. It will also be a valuable resource for adoption professionals.

Nurturing Adoptions
Creating Resilience after Neglect and Trauma
Deborah D. Gray
Paperback: £16.99 / $24.99
ISBN: 978 1 84905 891 9
512 pages

Adopted children who have suffered trauma and neglect have structural brain change, as well as specific developmental and emotional needs. They need particular care to build attachment and overcome trauma.

This book provides professionals with the knowledge and advice they need to help adoptive families build positive relationships and help children heal. It explains how neglect, trauma and prenatal exposure to drugs or alcohol affect brain and emotional development, and explains how to recognise these effects and attachment issues in children. It also provides ways to help children settle into new families and home and school approaches that encourage children to flourish. The book also includes practical resources such as checklists, questionnaires, assessments and tools for professionals including social workers, child welfare workers and mental health workers.

This book will be an invaluable resource for professionals working with adoptive families and will support them in nurturing positive family relationships and resilient, happy children. It is ideal as a child welfare text or reference book and will also be of interest to parents.

Attachment in Common Sense and Doodles
A Practical Guide
Miriam Silver
Paperback: £13.99 / $19.95
ISBN: 978 1 84905 314 3
208 pages

Attachment is a word used to describe a simple idea – the relationship with someone you love or whose opinions are important to you – so why is so much of the language relating to attachment so obscure, and why is it so challenging to help children who lack healthy attachment bonds?

Attachment in Common Sense and Doodles aims to bring some clarity and simplicity to the subject. Providing grounded information and advice accompanied by a series of simple 'doodles' throughout, it explains attachment in language that is easy to understand and describes how to apply this information in everyday life. It describes how the attachment patterns in children who are adopted or fostered differ, summarises the latest research in the field and provides advice on how to repair attachment difficulties and to build secure, loving relationships.

Covering all of the 'need to know' issues including how to spot attachment difficulties, build resilience and empathy and responding to problematic behaviour, this book will be an invaluable resource for families and professionals caring for children who are fostered, adopted or who have experienced early trauma.

Dr Miriam Silver is a Consultant Clinical Psychologist who specialises in parenting, attachment issues and the impact of early trauma. She has led a Child and Adolescent Mental Health Services team providing services for looked after and adopted children as well as conducting court expert witness work in Care proceedings. She holds two academic posts and has conducted research in risk and resilience factors in adoptive matching and the development, mental health and wellbeing of children who no longer live with their biological family. For several years she was chair of the national network of Clinical Psychologists working with Looked After and Adopted Children within the British Psychological Society.

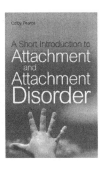

A Short Introduction to Attachment and Attachment Disorder
Colby Pearce
Paperback: £12.99 / $20.95
ISBN: 978 1 84310 957 0
112 pages
Part of the JKP 'Short Introductions' series

This book presents a short and accessible introduction to what 'attachment' means and how to recognise attachment disorders in children.

The author explains how complex problems in childhood may stem from the parent–child relationship during a child's early formative years, and later from the child's engagement with the broader social world. It explores the mindset of difficult and traumatised children and the motivations behind their apparently antisocial and defensive tendencies.

A Short Introduction to Attachment and Attachment Disorder includes case vignettes to illustrate examples, and offers a comprehensive set of tried-and-tested practical strategies for parents, carers and practitioners in supportive roles caring for children.

Colby Pearce is Principal Psychologist at Secure Start, a private psychology practice based in Adelaide that provides assessment and psychotherapy services in the areas of child protection, inter-country adoption, refugees and community child and family psychology. He has extensive experience in the teaching and training of psychologists and other professionals particularly in relation to insecure and attachment disordered children.